BUSINESS AFFAIRS

BUSINESS AFFAIRS

by John Chapman and Jeremy Lloyd

JOSEF WEINBERGER PLAYS

LONDON

BUSINESS AFFAIRS
First published in 2002
by Josef Weinberger Limited
12-14 Mortimer Street, London, W1T 3JJ

ISBN 0 85676 258 X

Printed by Watkiss Studios Ltd, Biggleswade, Beds, England

Business Affairs was first presented by Swallow Productions Ltd at the Mercury Theatre, Colchester, on 27 March 2001 prior to a national UK tour, with the following cast:

STANLEY BIGLEY	Ken Morley
NORMAN HARRIS	Gorden Kaye
HILDA BIGLEY	Vicki Michelle
ROSE HARRIS	Carol Harrison
KURT	Keith Drinkel
SVEN	Daniel Kruyer
SABRINA	Suzie Chard
VALERIE	Sally Chattaway

Directed by John B Hobbs
Lighting Design by Roger Frith
Production Manager Michael Tobyn
Produced by Stephen Beasley

CHARACTERS

in order of appearance

STANLEY BIGLEY

NORMAN HARRIS

HILDA BIGLEY

ROSE HARRIS

KURT

SVEN

SABRINA

VALERIE

Time: The present

The play takes place in a luxury suite of the Grand Hotel, Westminster, London.

ACT ONE

Evening in winter.

ACT TWO

The same.
The action is continuous.

ACT ONE

The action takes place in a luxury suite of the Grand Hotel, Westminster.

A central living room with doors to bedrooms off L and R. There is a centre archway and hallway which leads offstage R to the door to the corridor. To the L of the archway is a large window through which can be seen the skyline along the Thames.

The furnishings are elegant and consist of a sofa, an easy chair, desk, coffee table and minibar.

As the curtain rises STANLEY BIGLEY *is on the phone. He is a businessman from the North of England, in his forties, smartly dressed, and is the driving force in the partnership of Bigley & Harris, a truck haulage company in Huddersfield.*

STANLEY *is impatiently tapping his fingers.*

STANLEY   Ah, there you are. Flight arrivals? Didn't wake you did I? Did the flight arrive on time from Stuttgart? Oh . . . press one.

          (STANLEY *does so.*)

STANLEY   Press five.

          (STANLEY *does so. He now starts beating time to the music and humming some Vivaldi.*)

STANLEY   Ah. Flight arrivals, has the plane arrived from Stuttgart? S-T-U-er, uttgart.

          (NORMAN HARRIS *enters carrying a plastic bag with bottles. He is about the same age and of a nervous disposition.*)

NORMAN   I've got the champagne, Stanley.

STANLEY   Good.

(STANLEY *then speaks into phone.*)

STANLEY   Arrival confirmed. Thanks. And by the way I
            should change your music because ten minutes of
            Vivaldi can drive you mad.

            (NORMAN *puts the bottles in the fridge.*)

NORMAN   Was that the agency?

STANLEY   No, the airport. I was just making sure the eagle
            has landed. Kurt Hoffman and Sven Uberg are on
            their way as we speak.

NORMAN   Then for goodness sake get on to the agency.
            They were very insistent on us arranging some
            female company.

STANLEY   It's already done and paid for.

NORMAN   How did you find them?

            (STANLEY *picks up telephone book.*)

STANLEY   Yellow pages.

NORMAN   Under what?

STANLEY   Well it wasn't "Tools and Gardening."

NORMAN   I wouldn't know what to look for.

            (STANLEY *opens at the page.*)

STANLEY   "Escorts." Look, a whole page of them.

NORMAN   I hope they're reputable.

STANLEY   'Course they are. British Telecom wouldn't put
            rubbish in.

NORMAN   How did you know which one to pick?

STANLEY   I didn't. I took the first one that wasn't fully
            booked. It's Friday, you see. This one is "Classic
            Models". It guarantees a sophisticated female

companion will arrive at your door. Credit cards accepted.

NORMAN   Is it expensive?

STANLEY   How would I know? It's the first time I've ever ordered any.

NORMAN   How many have you ordered?

STANLEY   Two of course, one for Kurt and one for Sven.

NORMAN   How much?

STANLEY   Seven hundred and fifty quid.

(NORMAN *swallows*.)

NORMAN   A bit steep.

STANLEY   Each.

NORMAN   What!?

STANLEY   Calm down. It's not Huddersfield, it's London. They're very high class. It says here . . .

(STANLEY *points*.)

STANLEY   . . . "sophisticated" and sophisticated doesn't come cheap. It's a very small investment when you're doing a deal which can make us nearly three million quid for a fleet of trucks. Kurt and Sven will expect the best that England has to offer.

NORMAN   When do we pay?

STANLEY   We already have, I put it on your credit card.

NORMAN   Mine!?

STANLEY   I can't charge it to the company. It's not deductible. You're the accountant, you should know that. And Hilda goes through my statements with a fine-tooth comb.

NORMAN   What if Rose sees "'Classic Models" on mine?

STANLEY   Tell her it's for servicing a couple of old trucks.

NORMAN   The things you have to do to keep your head
           above water and not let on.

STANLEY   Hilda and Rose have no conception of what we
           have to go through to keep them in the manner
           they're accustomed to. Even now they'll be
           shopping to the last minute before catching the
           train back to Huddersfield.

NORMAN   I'm not so sure they're as keen as we are to sell up
           and live in Spain.

STANLEY   Then I'd say that's because they don't
           understand the ramifications of having money out
           of the country that's tax free.

NORMAN   Well, Rose has been talking lately about having
           second thoughts.

STANLEY   She what?

NORMAN   I mean she wonders how she'll cope with having
           nothing to do all day.

STANLEY   She's had plenty of practice, they both have, they
           don't do anything now.

NORMAN   Rose has her bell-ringing on Sundays.

STANLEY   It cost us enough when they got that whopping
           bell with the stupid name.

NORMAN   The Big Tom.

STANLEY   We're the Big Twits that subscribed for that.

NORMAN   We're pillars of the church.

STANLEY   I hope our prayers are noted on this deal. I could
           do with a drink.

NORMAN   Beer? Champagne?

STANLEY   Keep the champagne in the fridge, we'll only open
             that when the deal goes through. I'll have a
             whisky.

NORMAN   Right, and what shall I have?

STANLEY   We want you with a clear head, Norman, you'll
             have a tomato juice as usual.

             (NORMAN *goes to the minibar and fixes the drinks.*)

NORMAN   There's no justice.

STANLEY   You're dead right. You devote the best years of
             your life to build up the biggest trucking firm in
             Yorkshire and what happens? Up goes your
             vehicle excise duty, your fuel and your insurance
             and your profit goes out the window.

NORMAN   I can't see a light at the end of the tunnel. It's a
             sad fact, Stanley, we overstretched ourselves and
             if this sale doesn't go through we'll end up
             bankrupt.

STANLEY   Be positive. It will go through and what's more
             we'll be home and dry with our feet up in sunny
             Spain.

NORMAN   We could've been a bit premature putting that
             deposit on the apartments.

STANLEY   They sell like hot cakes. The Valparaiso Hill Club
             is one of the poshest addresses in Marbella.

NORMAN   We only put it down because we thought we'd
             sold to the Russians.

STANLEY   Lucky we found out it was dodgy money. But with
             a Swede and a German we're dealing with Anglo
             Saxons. We speak the same language.

NORMAN   We can't speak theirs.

STANLEY   We don't have to. They're educated.

(*The phone rings.* STANLEY *answers it.*)

STANLEY   Bigley here – oh Hilda, are you on the train? . . . In
          a taxi. Oh, on the way to King's Cross? . . . To
          here? You'll miss the train if you come here . . . Oh
          all right.

(STANLEY *turns to* NORMAN.)

She's bought a standard lamp – for Spain.

(STANLEY *speaks into the phone.*)

STANLEY   You could've waited till we'd got to Spain. They
          quite possibly sell them there . . . I see, well look,
          keep the taxi running, just leave it with the hall
          porter and Norman and I will bring it up in the
          Range Rover later . . . Bye love.

(STANLEY *replaces receiver.*)

STANLEY   They don't think do they? They do not think.

(*A mobile phone starts to ring.*)

STANLEY   Is that you or me?

(*They start looking for their briefcases.* NORMAN
finds his phone and answers it.)

NORMAN   It's mine. Mr Harris here . . . Oh Kurt – Guten Tag
          – yes, fine – ah – really . . . Splendid – right.

(NORMAN *switches his phone off.*)

STANLEY   Where are they, on the M4?

NORMAN   No South Bank, they took the helicopter.

STANLEY   Helicopter. They don't mind spending, do they,
          these Europeans.

NORMAN   But we're Europeans.

STANLEY   Yes, but we're English Europeans.

NORMAN   I've got a good feeling about this, Stanley.

STANLEY   Have you, Norman?

NORMAN   He sounded very eager on the phone. He thinks
           he's getting a bargain.

STANLEY   I'd say he was right. Thirty "headers and trailers"
           at eighty thousand pounds each gives us two
           point four million, tax free. And wisely invested
           gives us a not unreasonable lifestyle.

NORMAN   Plus the sale of the depot to that chain who want
           to build another supermarket for six hundred
           thousand.

STANLEY   Pity about the tax on that, but there we are.

NORMAN   Still, we walk away with a tidy sum. It's funny
           when you think how we started twenty years ago
           with a couple of delivery vans.

STANLEY   We had a bit of luck along the way, but we also
           had the will. Frankly, I think we're getting what we
           deserve. So let's drink to that, shall we?

NORMAN   Right.

STANLEY   Here's to La Dolce Vita.

NORMAN   Cheers.

           (*They drink.*)

STANLEY   And all those lovely golf courses.

NORMAN   Rose doesn't play golf.

STANLEY   She hasn't tried. Get her one of those practice
           things, you know, with a ball on the end of a
           string. She can tee it up on the balcony and whack
           it about 'til she gets the hang of it.

           (*He takes an imaginary drive.*)

STANLEY   Quatro!!

NORMAN	What's "Quatro" mean?
STANLEY	Spanish for "four".
NORMAN	It'll have to be after quatro o'clock, then.
STANLEY	Why?
NORMAN	With her skin she's got to keep in the shade 'til the heat goes out of the sun.
STANLEY	Rubbish. We've been to Spain a few times but I never knew that.
NORMAN	That's because you're playing golf all the time and you've never seen her in the middle of the day.
STANLEY	I must have.
NORMAN	But always under an umbrella, and you can't hold an umbrella and swing a golf club at the same time. That's all I'm saying.
STANLEY	Took long enough. Anyway I was talking to Hilda about investing in a boat.
NORMAN	Oh no. No, no – no.
STANLEY	Nothing too flash.
NORMAN	No, no, it's an inner-ear problem. She couldn't watch "The Cruel Sea" without taking Dramamine.
STANLEY	She can stand on the jetty and wave us goodbye with the umbrella.
NORMAN	I'd have to stay with her 'til she got used to the place, and could find where everything was, like the art galleries, and . . .
STANLEY	The coffee shop and the hairdresser's?
NORMAN	Yes.

(*The phone goes.*)

STANLEY	I suppose running with the bulls in Pamplona will be out of the question.

(STANLEY *speaks into phone.*)

Hello . . . Oh Hilda . . . You're coming up here. What for? . . .

(STANLEY *speaks to* NORMAN.)

STANLEY	They want to use the bathroom.

(STANLEY *speaks into phone.*)

STANLEY	No, it's all right, we haven't started the meeting yet, but make it quick.

(STANLEY *puts the phone down.*)

NORMAN	That was a bit abrupt.
STANLEY	We don't want them here when Kurt and Sven arrive. Once those women start talking you can't shut 'em up. They could easily say something that would scupper the deal.
NORMAN	Like what?
STANLEY	Like we're desperate men on the edge of bankruptcy.
NORMAN	Give them some credit, Stanley. They not stupid.
STANLEY	A couple of drinks and they could be. I don't want to take any chances. Now get those contracts out and let's check everything's in order.

(NORMAN *opens his briefcase.*)

NORMAN	Of course it's in order. That's my department.

(*Takes out the contracts and gives them to* STANLEY.)

NORMAN	All the I's are crossed and the T's dotted.

(STANLEY *glances at them.*)

STANLEY   Well, at least the names are spelt right.

NORMAN   All that's required now are the signatures and the
              date.

STANLEY   Hang on. We've overlooked something.

NORMAN   What?

STANLEY   It says here "witnesses". Who's going to witness
              the signatures?

NORMAN   We'll have witnesses.

STANLEY   Who?

NORMAN   The ladies we've got coming.

STANLEY   We can't have them for witnesses.

              (STANLEY *points to contract.*)

STANLEY   It says "occupation". What are they going to put
              down for that? Hookers?

NORMAN   You never said they were hookers.

STANLEY   Don't be so naive, what d'you think we've
              ordered, a couple of district nurses? They can't
              sign. We'll have to ask the manager up.

NORMAN   Not with those sort of women up here. What about
              our reputation?

STANLEY   They're for Kurt and Sven. They're not giving us
              one.

NORMAN   I should hope not. But they were ordered in my
              name. I hope they don't think I'm a participating
              party.

STANLEY   'Course not. Have you got clean underwear on?

NORMAN   Oh, cut it out, Stanley!

STANLEY	We'll have to go down to the manager's office for a signature.
NORMAN	Suppose we don't sign 'til after midnight, he might be in bed.
STANLEY	We'll get the hall porter and if he's not available I'll go out and get a policeman.
NORMAN	Not with hookers up here.
STANLEY	There's nothing illegal about this. Nobody knows what they are or that it's you who ordered them.
NORMAN	But I didn't!
STANLEY	I think you lack a little sophistication. Just leave it all to me.

(*The doorbell goes.* NORMAN *reacts.*)

NORMAN	Ah!

(STANLEY *goes off to open the door.*)

HILDA	(*off*) It's a posh lift.
STANLEY	(*entering*) Wait 'til you see the suite.

(HILDA *enters followed by* ROSE. *They're in their late thirties, good-looking and smartly dressed.* HILDA *is brisk and outgoing with dark hair, while* ROSE, *with fair hair, is more reserved and has attempted to refine her Yorkshire accent. She wears glasses.* HILDA *looks around.*)

HILDA	Oh – not bad. I quite like the wallpaper.
ROSE	Oh no! I wouldn't have chosen it, not with those curtains.
HILDA	You could be right.
STANLEY	We haven't time to redecorate, we've got a business meeting.

(ROSE *goes to* NORMAN *and gives him a little kiss on the head.*)

ROSE   Hello, pet!

STANLEY   Have you kept the taxi?

HILDA   No, the front desk is ordering us another one and
            there's a nice porter who's looking after our
            standard lamp, but we didn't leave this with him, it
            might've given him ideas.

            (HILDA *is pointing to* ROSE's *shopping bag.*)

STANLEY   Doesn't do much for me.

HILDA   Show him what's in it, Rose.

ROSE   No, I couldn't.

HILDA   Go on.

ROSE   Not in front of Stanley.

HILDA   He won't mind.

STANLEY   The suspense is killing me.

HILDA   Give it here.

            (HILDA *takes the bag and pulls out a nightie
            which she holds up.*)

HILDA   It was reduced.

NORMAN   By a couple of feet. Does it fit?

ROSE   Of course it fits.

NORMAN   It's a bit "dia*phee*nous".

ROSE   It was Hilda who pushed me into it.

HILDA   I told her it would be ideal for those hot steamy
            nights in Spain.

            (*She drapes it over a chair.*)

ROSE   (*to* NORMAN) I'll change it if you don't like it.

NORMAN   Oh no. I can just see you in that.

ROSE   Can you really?

NORMAN   Yes.

STANLEY   Stand in the windows and everyone will see you in it.

HILDA   Stanley, don't be vulgar.

ROSE   You look very tired, Norman.

NORMAN   Do I?

ROSE   You do, pet.

NORMAN   Well it's this deal, I'm under a lot of stress.

ROSE   Then may I suggest you don't drive home tonight? Sleep in this suite.

NORMAN   No, we can't!

STANLEY   No, you see Mr Hoffman and Mr Uberg are staying here tonight. That's why we've booked the suite.

HILDA   I hope all this is going to be worth it.

STANLEY   Worth it! This is the deal that's getting us out of Huddersfield and onto the Costa del Sol.

ROSE   I read it was very hot there yesterday. Wouldn't be surprised if people weren't dropping like flies.

NORMAN   Not if they've got air-conditioning and an umbrella. If you've got that then it'll be just as pleasant as our house.

ROSE   (*pause*) Then why are we moving?

STANLEY   Because we have to sell our company abroad, and keep the money abroad to avoid a swinging tax.

ROSE   Then why sell at all?

STANLEY   You'll have to know sooner or later. We're losing money hand over fist.

HILDA	We're not.
NORMAN	We are.
ROSE	You never told us.
HILDA	They never tell us anything.
ROSE	No wonder you've got that strained look. Is there anything else we should know?
NORMAN	No, nothing.
ROSE	You mustn't bottle things up. You would tell me, wouldn't you?
NORMAN	Of course I would.
HILDA	I realise now, Rose, why you had that terrible time in Harrods just now with the Visa people.
NORMAN	Visa?
ROSE	I wanted to buy a handbag. I gave them our card number and apparently we've just spent fifteen hundred pounds.
NORMAN	Have we?
ROSE	Yes.
HILDA	What've you spent it on?
NORMAN	(*to* STANLEY) What have I spent it on?
STANLEY	Don't you remember?
NORMAN	(*desperate*) No, of course I don't!
STANLEY	He paid for the suite.
ROSE	Oh well, that explains it.
HILDA	No it doesn't. If they've charged you fifteen hundred pounds for one night you've been diddled. Stanley, we'll go and see the manager.

STANLEY	No it wasn't for one night, it was for two nights in case we couldn't settle it all tonight. But of course if it's settled then we get a refund.
HILDA	It's still seven hundred and fifty pounds a night. That's outrageous. We've never paid more than four hundred anywhere.
NORMAN	Ah, but it's the extras you see.
HILDA	Such as what?
NORMAN	Er . . .

(NORMAN *looks at* STANLEY.)

STANLEY	Bowl of fruit, flowers, a view of Big Ben.
NORMAN	Full central heating.
STANLEY	And full central heating.
ROSE	That couldn't come to three hundred and fifty pounds.
NORMAN	Plus bath-gel and shower caps.
ROSE	I'm phoning the manager.

(ROSE *goes to phone.* NORMAN *stops her.*)

NORMAN	No you're not!
ROSE	What's making you so edgy?
STANLEY	It's this deal, Rose, we're on a knife edge.
ROSE	I'd no idea things were so bad.
HILDA	Look, Stanley, we don't want to ruin our lives for the sake of money, it's not worth it. If you can't sell the business we'll forget about Spain. I'd be quite happy to settle for a little flat in Bournemouth.
ROSE	My Auntie Peggy lives there.

STANLEY   Norman and I have set our sights on Spain and
             God willing that's where we're going to be, with a
             load of cash in the bank. Which is better than
             being broke in Bournemouth, with or without your
             Auntie Peggy.

HILDA   Is there anything we can do to help?

STANLEY   Yes. Try not to do any shopping between here and
             the station.

             (*The phone goes.*)

HILDA   That'll be the porter, telling me he's got a cab, not
             easy in this weather.

             (HILDA *picks up the receiver.*)

HILDA   Hello, who's that? Classic Models . . . Oh sounds
             like a very old fashioned taxi . . . I beg your
             pardon? The ladies have cancelled? No, we
             haven't cancelled . . . Sabrina and Valerie have
             cancelled.

             (NORMAN *is standing looking like a stuck pig.*)

HILDA   Are you sure you've got the right room? Thirty-
             three, yes. But who exactly requested the company
             of Sabrina and Valerie? A Mr Harris – I see.

             (STANLEY *mops his brow.*)

             And he'll get a refund? . . . As much as that. Yes,
             I'll certainly tell him, and his next of kin.

             (HILDA *replaces the receiver.*)

ROSE   Who was that?

HILDA   That, Rose, was an escort agency with news that
             Sabrina and Valerie are unable to fulfil their
             engagement for Mr Harris.

ROSE   An escort agency? It must be a mistake.

HILDA	Me answering the phone was the mistake.
ROSE	There must be another Mr Harris.
HILDA	Not another Mr Harris who's going to get fifteen hundred pounds refund on his credit card.
NORMAN	It's not what you think.
HILDA	It's what we know. Your husband has ordered a couple of tarts, dear.
NORMAN	I didn't. He did.
ROSE	(*to* STANLEY) And you put them on Norman's credit card.
STANLEY	They're not for him and they're not for me.
HILDA	Oh, don't give us that.
STANLEY	As Norman is my witness we have a fax from Kurt Hoffman and Sven Uberg requesting female companions for the evening.
NORMAN	I've got the fax here.
STANLEY	Get it out. Show it to them and make them eat their words.
	(NORMAN *gets it out of the briefcase and points.*)
NORMAN	There you are. Bottom of the page.
	(ROSE *moves glasses onto the end of her nose.*)
ROSE	Let me see . . . "and arrange if you please two ladies for dining, etc . . . and if the deal is concluded between us we will reimburse you for any extra expenses incurred for this request. PS: If possible one blonde, one brunette." Well – would you believe it?
HILDA	Yes I would. You read about this sort of thing in the papers.

ROSE   But you don't expect your husbands to be caught
            up in it.

STANLEY   We're not caught up in it, you silly –

HILDA   (*quickly*) Stanley!

NORMAN   And they're not even coming, so there's nothing
            to worry about.

HILDA   Not now, no, but five minutes ago there was. No
            wonder you said don't bother to come up.

ROSE   She was dying to powder her nose.

STANLEY   Well, she hasn't done it yet. It's through there.

            (STANLEY *points to the door.*)

HILDA   I'd forgotten all about it.

            (HILDA *starts to go then quickly turns.*)

HILDA   The point is, if I hadn't answered the phone we
            wouldn't have known what you were getting up to.

STANLEY   We were merely complying with an overseas
            request.

ROSE   I'm surprised at you, Norman.

NORMAN   So am I.

STANLEY   I don't condone this sort of thing any more than
            you do, but if it helps to oil the wheels of industry
            and if it means our financial survival then so be it.
            This is normal business practice today. You know
            Gerald Walters at the golf club, he was telling me
            the last time he was in Tokyo for the wool
            conference, the first night they had half a dozen
            geisha girls waving their fans about.

ROSE   Not Gerald Walters?

STANLEY   Yes.

ROSE   But he's in our bell-ringing team.

STANLEY	What's that got to do with it?
ROSE	I shall look at him in a new light.
STANLEY	It's all perfectly harmless, that's just the way the Japanese entertain.
NORMAN	You know what they say, "when in Rome".
HILDA	Oh I see, and what about when you're in Stockholm?
ROSE	And Strutgart? (*Sic.*)
STANLEY	Those were bona fide meetings with Kurt and Sven to set this whole deal up.
HILDA	And were you offered the same services?
STANLEY } NORMAN	No. Yes.
HILDA	You what?
STANLEY } NORMAN	Yes. No.
HILDA	Well – which?
STANLEY	Naturally being important businessmen it was on the table.
NORMAN	(*puzzled*) Was it? I never saw it.
STANLEY	I mean it was suggested, but being a happily married man I said "No".
ROSE	(*to* NORMAN) And what did you say?
NORMAN	I said "Yes".
ROSE	Norman!
NORMAN	I said, "Yes, I'm happily married as well."
HILDA	I don't know what to believe.

STANLEY   Why can't you take my word for it?

HILDA   I don't think your word is worth that! (*Clicks finger.*) You've been very underhand.

STANLEY   I'm being dead honest. I've told you about the girls.

HILDA   You wouldn't have done if I hadn't picked up that phone.

STANLEY   You wouldn't have picked it up if you hadn't been going to the bathroom.

HILDA   Oh drat, yes.

           (*She starts to go towards bedroom again and stops and turns.*)

HILDA   And another thing –

STANLEY   Here we go . . .

HILDA   Rose and I are not leaving the hotel until this deal is signed and sealed.

ROSE   Aren't we?

HILDA   Don't you see, as soon as our backs are turned they'll be on that phone ordering two more.

ROSE   They wouldn't!

HILDA   They would.

NORMAN   We wouldn't. They're fully booked. Stanley tried them all.

HILDA   Oh, did he?

NORMAN   Well, you see it's Friday, it's their busy night!

STANLEY   Oh, shut up!

HILDA   You're a dark one, you are.

STANLEY   Give over.

HILDA   I can't believe you sat there ringing up girls and giving out it was for Norman.

STANLEY   I never said it was for Norman.

HILDA   You said it was for you, did you?

STANLEY   No. I said that two highly respectable businessmen, one German, one Swede, required the company of two charming and elegant lady companions for dinner.

ROSE   One blonde and one brunette.

STANLEY   I don't remember being that specific. It was just that we wanted ladies with proper class.

ROSE   I doubt you'd find many ladies of class doing that.

STANLEY   On the contrary, I've read that some respectable widows and even married women earn a little extra money by having an evening out with a lonely gentleman.

NORMAN   There's plenty of those about.

HILDA   There could be two more soon.

ROSE   Well, I don't think any married ladies would do that in Huddersfield.

HILDA   Have you noticed Mrs Holroyd always closes the bedroom curtains in the afternoon.

ROSE   The chemist told me she has a very bad migraine.

STANLEY   I don't want to seem abrupt, but we have a meeting to conduct here, one that's a matter of life and death, which could affect all our futures, and you're rabbiting on about Mrs Bloody Holroyd's migraine.

NORMAN   I think I'm getting one myself.

HILDA   Then I suggest the sooner you book our rooms
            the better. And make sure you get them on this
            landing.

STANLEY   If you insist.

HILDA   Go on, do it now. Pick up the phone.

STANLEY   Why don't you?

HILDA   'Cos I'm going to the bathroom.

            (HILDA *turns to go.* STANLEY *picks up the phone.*)

STANLEY   (*listening*) Reception is engaged.

            (HILDA *turns back.*)

HILDA   It would be. Well, nip down and do it at the desk.

STANLEY   Tell you what. Why don't you wear my trousers,
            order the room and do the deal yourself.

HILDA   And don't think I couldn't. You and I are going to
            have a very serious discussion when we get home.

STANLEY   Carry on like that and I might not come home at all.
            I won't be dictated to in front of our friends.

NORMAN   (*helpfully*) It's all right, we don't mind.

STANLEY   I mind. Come on Norman, let's sort these rooms
            out.

NORMAN   We can't use my credit card.

STANLEY   We'll charge it up to the company.

NORMAN   Under what?

STANLEY   "Staff Outing."

            (*They exit.*)

ROSE   They've got a cheek.

HILDA   Did you have any inkling about this?

ROSE   The lady escorts?

HILDA   No, the business being on the rocks.

ROSE   No, it hasn't sunk in yet.

HILDA   I mean, for the past ten years we've never wanted for anything. I can't face going back to where we started.

ROSE   We're going to have a sleepless night wondering if the deal's going through.

HILDA   You take your lifestyle for granted, don't you? But suddenly it could all be taken away.

ROSE   What about those lovely apartments in Marbella? If we can't complete on those we'll lose the deposit.

HILDA   I wasn't all that keen 'til now, but the thought of losing them makes me more depressed. D'you think we've been a bit hard on our husbands?

ROSE   Well, you have. I feel almost sorry for Norman, he was really doing it on my behalf because he wants to keep me in comfort.

HILDA   I suppose to be honest the same goes for my Stanley. We'd never have known what a crisis we were facing if we hadn't come up here. I think it was fate.

ROSE   No dear, it was the bathroom.

HILDA   Oh Lord, yes!

            (*Hurries off to the bedroom.*)

HILDA   Should be one in here.

            (*Exits to the bedroom R.*)

ROSE   Hurry! I want to go as well!

HILDA   (*off*) Try the other bedroom!

ROSE   Oh, right.

             (*She exits to the bedroom L.*)

KURT   (*off*) Thank you. We'll take the bags.

             (KURT *enters. Tanned, good-looking, fortyish and
             expensively dressed. His accent only adds to his
             charm. He is carrying a soft holdall.*)

SVEN   (*off*) Kurt, have you any change?

KURT   After the taxi, the doorman, the hall porter, I've
             run out. Tell him we'll tip him when we leave.

SVEN   (*off*) Thank you for your help.

             (SVEN *enters. He is equally smart, handsome and
             fortyish.*)

SVEN   Nice room!

KURT   I need a drink. How about you?

             (*Goes to the minibar.*)

SVEN   Beer would be fine.

KURT   Not too much, though. We need clear heads for
             the meeting.

SVEN   I think they're asking too much.

KURT   I'm sure we can get a reduction.

SVEN   Bigley is a tough cookie.

KURT   Concentrate on Harris. He's the weak one.

SVEN   Let's hope at least they have arranged some
             decent females, because we don't want to waste
             all night arguing about stupid trucks.

             (KURT *sees the nightie and holds it up.*)

KURT	This looks promising.
SVEN	Oh! They must be here already.
	(*They are now drinking their beers.*)
KURT	Obviously reliable. A good sign I think.
SVEN	I specifically asked for one blonde and one brunette.
KURT	Have you a preference?
SVEN	Yes indeed, I prefer blondes, providing it's a matching set.
KURT	Fine by me.
SVEN	This bit is always exciting. Wondering what you're going to get.
	(HILDA *enters and is surprised to see the men.*)
HILDA	Oh, pardon me. I didn't know you'd arrived. You must be the gentlemen we're expecting.
KURT	And you must be one of the ladies we're expecting.
HILDA	I beg your pardon?
	(KURT *holds up the nightie.*)
KURT	Could this naughty little number be yours?
HILDA	No, it's not, it belongs to my friend.
KURT	Tell me, is she by any chance a blonde?
HILDA	Well, yes, as a matter of fact she is.
KURT	(*to* SVEN) Your luck is holding.
HILDA	Give me that. I've got something to explain.
KURT	We don't need any explanation.

HILDA	No, but I think my friend might.

(ROSE *enters*.)

ROSE	The beds look ever so comfy . . .

(ROSE *stops on seeing the men*.)

ROSE	Oh, pardon me.
HILDA	Never mind the beds, we've got a problem. I was just telling them about your nightie being left lying around by mistake.
ROSE	Oh, forgive me, it shouldn't have been there.
SVEN	Nothing to forgive. May I know your name?
ROSE	Rose.
SVEN	I'm Uberg. Sven Uberg.

(*He kisses her hand*.)

ROSE	You must be the one from Sweden.
SVEN	Yes.
HILDA	(*aside*) I need a quick word with you.
KURT	(*refers to* HILDA) And what's this divine creature's name?
ROSE	This is Hilda.
KURT	Hilda. Would that be short for Hildegard?
HILDA	Er . . . no.
KURT	Never mind. I shall call you Hildegard. I once knew a Hildegard who had beautiful legs – like yours.
HILDA	Did I? – Have you? I mean –
ROSE	Aren't they complimentary?
HILDA	Yes, but I still need a word with you.

KURT	(*to* HILDA) By the way my name is Kurt.
HILDA	Kurt, yes, very nice. Now I think I need to tell you something about me and Rose. We don't do what you think.
KURT	Oh, so you have some surprises in store for us. Always happy to experiment.
HILDA	Oh, heck.
	(KURT *looks at his watch.*)
KURT	It's getting late. Give us a moment to shower and freshen up. (*Picks up his case.*) I'll take this room. (*Exits.*)
SVEN	That's fine by me.
ROSE	I like the name Sven.
SVEN	Oh, really?
ROSE	You don't hear it often. The only one I've come across is Svengali.
SVEN	(*laughs*) Svengali, I don't think he was Swedish.
ROSE	He could hypnotise girls, you know.
SVEN	It's a trait of Svens.
	(*He slowly removes* ROSE'S *glasses, hands them to her and gives her a seductive stare. He exits with his case, leaving* ROSE *looking like a hypnotised rabbit.*)
HILDA	(*grabs* ROSE) What are you thinking of?
ROSE	What have I said?
HILDA	Stop leading them on.
ROSE	I was just being polite.
HILDA	What you don't know is that they think we're the tarts from the agency.

ROSE   Sabrina and Valerie?

HILDA   Yes!

ROSE   I said my name was Rose.

HILDA   They don't know their names.

ROSE   But we don't look like tarts do we? This outfit
            came from Harvey Nichols.

HILDA   At seven hundred and fifty pounds a night, they
            can afford Harvey Nichols.

ROSE   What made you think they've mistaken us?

HILDA   Because before you came back he had your nightie
            in his hand telling me how pleased he was to see
            that the "lady escorts" had arrived.

ROSE   Why didn't you tell him the truth?

HILDA   I was about to when you barged in.

ROSE   Well, we'll straighten it out for them when they
            come back. It's easy to see how they made the
            mistake. They're obviously expecting two very
            elegant ladies. It'll be quite a disappointment for
            them when we explain the mistake. He was quite
            complimentary about your legs.

HILDA   Quite? D'you mind? He was very complimentary.
            A man of the world. You could tell by the way he
            was dressed.

ROSE   I've given up on Norman.

HILDA   We'll have a tale to tell our circle when we get
            back.

ROSE   I don't think it's something we should mention.

HILDA   Why not?

ROSE   It's hardly something to be proud of.

HILDA   I can't wait to see Stanley's face when I tell him that a man of Kurt's calibre thinks I'm a femme fatale.

ROSE   You're not a femme fatale dear, you're seven hundred and fifty quid. I wonder if that was all in?

HILDA   That's something we shall never know.

ROSE   I meant "inclusive", Hilda.

         (KURT *appears with a towel round his waist and an aerosol deodorant in his hand. He is showing off his bronzed physique.*)

KURT   Before the evening begins I think I should acquaint you with the bare facts.

HILDA   I think we should acquaint you with ours.

KURT   All in good time. You see we are here to deal with two rather boring businessmen from the North who are trying to sell us some vehicles. They are very heavy going, but try and laugh if they make a joke and make sure their glasses are always full. Then as soon as we have managed to beat them down to the lowest figure, we shall sign, get rid of them, and the fun begins.

         (*He sprays quickly under his arms, pulls the towel away from his stomach and gives a squirt to the lower regions. He then exits to the bedroom.*)

HILDA   Did you hear that? Two boring men from the North.

ROSE   What a cheek. You'd never say my Norman was boring would you?

HILDA   (*slight pause*) No – quiet maybe.

ROSE   He has his moments.

HILDA   I'm sure he has. And what about all that keeping
             the glasses filled. They want to get them tiddly so
             they'll get the business cheap.

ROSE   Very underhand.

HILDA   I'm damned if we're going to let them short-
             change our husbands.

ROSE   How can we stop it?

HILDA   By staying in this suite, having dinner and being
             what they think we are.

ROSE   Ladies of the night?

HILDA   This night, yes. That penny I spent has probably
             saved us a lot of money.

ROSE   I'm sorry, I couldn't. It's not in my nature.

HILDA   You don't think it's in mine, do you?

ROSE   No, of course not, but you're more outgoing than I
             am, and you've got the legs for it.

HILDA   Rubbish. Who can't wait to be in amateur
             dramatics?

ROSE   That's different, you're not yourself, you're
             playing a part.

HILDA   That's what we'd be doing here. I'll never forget
             you in the Christmas revue playing that vamp.

ROSE   Now you mention it I did get a good write-up in
             the *Yorkshire Evening Post*.

             (STANLEY *enters*.)

STANLEY   It's no good, every room in the hotel is booked
             up. Norman's hanging on trying to get a taxi for
             you.

HILDA   There's no need.

STANLEY	There is. I Don't want you here when our Baltic Transport friends arrive.
HILDA	I've got news for you, love, they're already here.
	(STANLEY *looks round.*)
STANLEY	Where?
ROSE	They're freshening up in their rooms.
STANLEY	I hope they're not too disappointed when we tell them we don't have any female companions.
HILDA	Oh, but they do.
STANLEY	Don't tell me they brought their own.
HILDA	No, they found two.
STANLEY	Where?
HILDA	Here, in this hotel.
STANLEY	Bit of luck. Have you seen them?
HILDA	Yes, and so have you.
STANLEY	What do they look like?
HILDA	We'll give you a hint. Rose, give us one of your poses.
	(ROSE *lounges against the sofa and lifts her skirt a little.*)
ROSE	(*á la Mae West*) "Come up and see me sometime".
STANLEY	Come off it, Rose. What the hell's going on?
HILDA	I'll tell you what. Those men walked in here and mistook us for the girls from the agency.
STANLEY	Never.
HILDA	I'll give you "never".
STANLEY	What I mean is, it's an insult isn't it?

ROSE   Why? They were expecting two attractive women
              probably not quite as smart and sophisticated as
              me and Hilda, but as far as they were concerned
              that was a bonus.

STANLEY   I'd chuck them out if we weren't doing business
              with them.

HILDA   Pretty funny business, too.

STANLEY   What d'you mean?

HILDA   Before we could straighten them out as to who we
              were, they let slip their plans for how they were
              going to handle the meeting.

STANLEY   And how's that?

HILDA   They're going to make sure you have too much to
              drink, get you tiddly so they can knock the price
              down.

ROSE   And it's up to us to keep topping your glasses up.

STANLEY   Crafty buggers.

HILDA   Right. So we can be just as crafty and get them
              tiddly.

STANLEY   Hilda, be reasonable. With the best will in the
              world, who's going to believe you're those sort of
              women? You couldn't carry it off. You just look
              like normal housewives.

HILDA   Have you seen a normal housewife walk like this?

              (*She walks with an exaggerated sway of the hips.*)

STANLEY   Not unless they need a hip replacement.

HILDA   You'll be sorry you said that.

STANLEY   I will not have any wife of mine lounging on the
              sofa saying "Come up and see me some time".

ROSE   You said the girls were just elegant company for lonely men at a business dinner, nothing about flaunting bodies.

STANLEY   Elegant company doesn't keep lying on the sofa saying, "Come up and see me sometime".

ROSE   I was just showing you that I could be sexy.

STANLEY   If that's seven hundred and fifty quid's worth you're overcharging.

HILDA   Stanley, don't be rude. Rose got a very good write-up for doing that in the *Yorkshire Evening Post*.

STANLEY   If she gets a write-up for this it'll be in the *News of the World*.

HILDA   Typical. You're all mouth and trousers. When it comes to something important like this you bottle out. Thank your lucky stars you've got us behind you to help.

STANLEY   Right, I'll grant you you've done your bit warning us about the drink, so we'll stay sober.

ROSE   Let me set the scene for you while you're all discussing terms. I shall be gazing into Sven's eyes and while he's totally mesmerised I shall be topping up his drink.

STANLEY   Will you be wearing your glasses?

ROSE   Certainly not.

STANLEY   It'll be all over the table, you're as blind as a bat.

            (KURT *enters in trousers but no shirt.*)

KURT   Can you bring me a beer, Hildegard?

STANLEY   Who's Hildegard?

HILDA   Me, it's my professional name.

KURT   Oh, hello Stanley, be with you soon. Won't be
            long. And by the way, the ladies, an excellent
            choice. Sophisticated, mature. Quite a change from
            those bimbos in Stuttgart.

            (*He exits.*)

HILDA   What bimbos are those?

STANLEY   They weren't with us, they were with them.

HILDA   Your nose is getting longer.

            (*She does her sexy walk to pick up the beer and
            then goes into the bedroom.*)

KURT   Hildegard!

HILDA   Coming Kurt.

            (*She exits.*)

STANLEY   I think our marriage could be in jeopardy.

ROSE   It's a problem a lot of bimbos are at the bottom of.

            (SVEN *appears at the door.*)

SVEN   Be with you in a minute, a button's come off my
            shirt!

ROSE   Don't worry, I'll sew it on for you. There'll be kit
            in there.

SVEN   Thank you, my dear.

            (*Exits.* ROSE *slinks to the door.*)

STANLEY   It's only a button, don't wear your motor out.

            (ROSE *exits as* NORMAN *comes in from the hall.*)

NORMAN   No sign of a taxi but the porter's told me that our
            business friends have arrived.

STANLEY   Correct. Now I've got some good news and some bad news.

NORMAN   Oh, what's the good news?

STANLEY   We've found two escort ladies.

NORMAN   Spot on. What's the bad news?

STANLEY   We're married to them.

NORMAN   Come again?

STANLEY   In our absence Kurt and Sven have mistook our wives for fifteen hundred pounds worth of nooky.

NORMAN   Never. Not Rose, surely.

STANLEY   Even Rose.

NORMAN   Why didn't they point out the mistake?

STANLEY   That avenue was gone down but before they got to the end of it, it transpired that the Baltic Transport Company let slip the fact that they hope to diddle us by encouraging the girls to get us pissed.

NORMAN   That's typical of foreigners.

STANLEY   Very nobly our wives are prepared to sacrifice themselves.

NORMAN   Rose would never agree to that.

STANLEY   Don't be too sure. Five minutes ago she was draped round the sofa doing a Mae West!

NORMAN   It's awful.

STANLEY   It's not too hot, I grant you.

NORMAN   No, I mean she only does that for me on my birthday.

STANLEY   Just pray it's not Sven's birthday.

NORMAN   Where is he?

STANLEY   In there with your wife.

NORMAN   So where's Hilda?

STANLEY   In there with Kurt. And by the way, please note
           she's working under her professional name,
           Hildegard.

NORMAN   It's enough to drive you to drink.

STANLEY   No, you mustn't! That's what they're after. We've
           got to stay sober.

NORMAN   I can't let my wife demean herself.

STANLEY   Norman, our lives, our very lives are on the brink
           here. Can you face poverty again?

NORMAN   Could I face riches knowing what my wife had to
           do to get it?

STANLEY   She hasn't done a damn thing except sew a button
           on.

NORMAN   Where?

STANLEY   In the bedroom.

NORMAN   Was it a trouser button?

STANLEY   Who cares?

NORMAN   I do!

STANLEY   You're over-reacting. It's just a button.

NORMAN   It may be a button now, but you know what these
           men will be expecting from our wives later on.

STANLEY   All they have to do is to say they have a
           headache.

NORMAN   You're right. It's never failed yet.

           (SVEN *enters*.)

SVEN Stanley, hello.

STANLEY How d'you do, Sven?

SVEN Nice to see you and Norman.

(Shakes hands.)

NORMAN Hello.

SVEN What a dirty night.

NORMAN Eh?

SVEN All this raining, plays merry hell with the traffic. A helicopter is the only answer. Let's have some drinks.

STANLEY No, we're fine thanks.

SVEN Nonsense, this is a night for celebration.

STANLEY All right then, let's sign and celebrate.

SVEN I think Kurt has some little adjustments to suggest on the price.

STANLEY Has he, we'll see about that. Get him in and we'll discuss it.

SVEN No rush, we've got all night. And talking of night you have chosen some delightful ladies for us.

NORMAN Have we?

SVEN I would say the top end of the market.

STANLEY That's very complimentary, isn't it Norman?

NORMAN Very.

SVEN This one I have, the blonde, Rose, did you pick her personally?

STANLEY No, we've never clapped eyes on her, have we Norman?

NORMAN   No.

STANLEY   We just phoned a top agency and said we want the best you've got.

SVEN   Well, I can't answer for the brunette but my Rosie is quite unusual.

NORMAN   In what way?

SVEN   She's not just a pretty face, she does extras.

NORMAN   Extras!?

SVEN   First she sews a button on and then she finds a little hole in my sweater.

NORMAN   Really.

STANLEY   Sporting of her, isn't it Norman?

SVEN   Such a change from the younger ones. Although she's more mature you can see there's a fire burning inside there.

STANLEY   Let's hope she doesn't set the smoke alarm off, eh Norman?

NORMAN   Yes.

SVEN   You must meet her. (*Calls out.*) Rosie! Come and join us. (*To* STANLEY *and* NORMAN.) When you see her tell me how attractive you think she is on a scale of one to ten. Frankly, I'd give her eight plus.

            (SVEN *holds up eight fingers.* ROSE *enters holding the sweater which she is sewing.*)

ROSE   Hang on Sven, I'm just finishing.

SVEN   Time for you to be introduced to our business associates.

ROSE   I won't be a moment.

(*She exits, biting off the thread.*)

SVEN   What d'you think?

NORMAN   Oh, definitely nine.

              (NORMAN *holds up nine fingers.*)

SVEN   Stanley?

STANLEY   Oh . . .

              (STANLEY *holds up five fingers.*)

NORMAN   (*offended*) Is that all? Five?

STANLEY   That's just for presentation. I dare say the
              "performance" would be ten.

SVEN   I will let you know. I think she has deep waters.
              Was she expensive?

STANLEY   Yes, but don't even think about it. It's our treat,
              isn't it Norman?

NORMAN   It would appear so.

              (ROSE *enters.*)

ROSE   I've put it back in the case on top of your 'Y'
              fronts.

SVEN   Thank you, quite the housewife. We have a saying
              in Sweden that you should have a wife in the
              kitchen and a tart in the bedroom.

STANLEY   (*laughs*) Very funny. Come on Norman, where's
              your sense of humour?

              (NORMAN *gives a false laugh.*)

SVEN   Rosie, come and meet Mr Bigley and Mr Harris.

ROSE   Which is which?

STANLEY   I'm Stanley Bigley, and this is my associate,
              Norman Harris.

ROSE   How d'you do, Mr Bigley?

STANLEY   How d'you do?

ROSE   Mr Harris?

NORMAN   That's me.

ROSE   Oh, you're the one that booked us.

NORMAN   We both booked, but it was my card.

ROSE   Lovely. Have you used the agency before?

NORMAN   No!

STANLEY   This is his first time.

ROSE   You're a naughty boy, aren't you?

NORMAN   No!

            (NORMAN *grabs her hand.*)

NORMAN   I promise you.

SVEN   Hands off, Norman, this little cracker is all mine.
            You wait until yours arrives.

ROSE   Have you ordered a couple as well?

NORMAN   No!

STANLEY   Rose! How could you say such a thing. We're
            married.

ROSE   Does that make a difference?

SVEN   Why should it? I'm married.

ROSE   Happily?

SVEN   How can you say what is happiness? At the
            beginning yes, but after a few years, a couple of
            children, the excitement goes and life becomes a
            little boring.

ROSE   I can imagine.

SVEN   But in Sweden, the men got together and we have
            a wonderful time. I belong to the "Iron Man" Club.

STANLEY   Is that golf?

SVEN   The "Iron Men" get up at six in the morning, strip
            off naked, dive into the lake, swim for two miles,
            climb out and run for ten miles, then mount
            bicycles and ride home.

ROSE   What, still naked?

SVEN   No, we have little shorts in our saddlebags. Then
            we all see who can drink the most Schnapps
            without falling down.

STANLEY   Is there any point to this club?

SVEN   Oh yes, the winner gets an "Iron Man's" hat.

NORMAN   He bloody deserves it.

SVEN   I've won three times.

STANLEY   I'll take your word for it.

SVEN   Don't take my word, I have one in my case. It's a
            sign of my stamina and impresses the ladies. I
            wear it at parties and the ladies fall over
            themselves. I will show you. When you're an "Iron
            Man" you're never without it.

            (SVEN *exits to the bedroom.*)

ROSE   Don't they lead an active life in Sweden?

NORMAN   You don't have to act common, Rose.

STANLEY   She's got a part to play.

ROSE   I thought you'd've realised that, pet.

NORMAN   You're egging him on.

            (KURT *enters with* HILDA.)

KURT   Has Rose introduced herself to you gentlemen?

STANLEY   Oh yes, very charming . . .

KURT   You haven't met Hildegard.

HILDA   I haven't had the pleasure yet.

STANLEY   I'm delighted to hear it.

KURT   This is Mr Bigley and Mr Harris.

HILDA   Oh Mr Harris, you're the one who . . .

NORMAN   (*cutting in*) Booked you, yes.

KURT   Have you girls worked together before?

HILDA   Oh yes, we've made quite a name for ourselves.

KURT   What name is this?

HILDA   The er . . . the "Dream Team".

STANLEY   The dream team?

KURT   Splendid. Perhaps you will make some of mine
            come true.

HILDA   Depends on what they are.

KURT   There is one I have always thought would be fun.

STANLEY   Oh! (*Worried.*) Would you care to share it with us?

KURT   No. But I will share it with Hildegard. (*To* HILDA.)
            May I whisper?

HILDA   I'm all ears.

            (KURT *whispers in her ear. Her eyes get wider and
            wider. Then* KURT *finishes.*)

HILDA   You've got to be fit for that.

ROSE   What? What was it?

HILDA	I'd rather not say.
KURT	She's part of the team. Maybe she'd like it, too.
HILDA	I don't think so.
ROSE	Let me be the judge.
NORMAN	No, Rose. You'd better not know. She's very shy.
KURT	How do you know? You've never met her.
STANLEY	That's true.
NORMAN	I mean, she looks shy.
KURT	Looking shy is what makes her so desirable.
ROSE	Oh Kurt, thank you. Now tell me Hildegard, what did he fancy?

(HILDA *whispers in her ear.*)

ROSE	Rather you than me.
HILDA	Certainly one for the book.
KURT	Care to have a trial run, Hildegard?
STANLEY	Steady on Kurt, first things first, business before pleasure. We've got a deal to sign. You can try it later.
KURT	Very well, pour the drinks.
NORMAN	Not for me thanks.
KURT	Rubbish. I never trust a man who doesn't drink. Let us fill our glasses.
HILDA	Shall I pour?
KURT	No, no. Sven has brought some Schnapps.
NORMAN	I don't think that would agree with me.
ROSE	Perhaps he's one of those men who can't drink on an empty stomach.

KURT	Then let's get some food inside him. What are we eating?
STANLEY	We're having it up here. I've ordered a cold collation. I hope that's all right?
KURT	Get them to send it up now.
STANLEY	Right.

(STANLEY *goes to phone.*)

STANLEY	It's an assortment you know, sausages, vol-au-vents, canapes. (*Sic.*)
KURT	Perhaps our ladies are vegetarian.
NORMAN	No, they're not.
KURT	How d'you know?
NORMAN	I mean they couldn't be. Look at the size of that one. (*Indicates* HILDA.)
HILDA	You can talk, with your stomach hanging over your belt.
STANLEY	We haven't paid you to be rude, you know.

(STANLEY *speaks into the phone.*)

STANLEY	Room Service? You can send up the dinner now. . .
KURT	Ask for some grapes . . .
STANLEY	Oh.

(STANLEY *speaks into phone.*)

STANLEY	Could you manage some grapes? Would you like anything, Norman?
NORMAN	Some prunes and custard.
STANLEY	Could you manage some prunes and custard?

KURT	(*to* HILDA) I can lie back on the bed and you can feed them to me one by one.
HILDA	Prunes and custard?
KURT	No. Grapes.
STANLEY	Make it a big bunch. Thanks.
	(STANLEY *puts the phone down*.)
HILDA	You like being mollycoddled, don't you?
KURT	I shall be naked, except for a sheet.
HILDA	You and your fantasies. What will you think of next?
STANLEY	Don't encourage him.
KURT	You see. I've made you jealous.
STANLEY	Just a little, maybe.
KURT	It's a pity you didn't order one of these for yourself.
STANLEY	That thought constantly crosses my mind.
NORMAN	Except we wouldn't, because we're married.
KURT	What does your wife look like?
NORMAN	Oh-er-er-well-er-er ...
ROSE	Have you forgotten?
NORMAN	No.
KURT	Blonde, brunette, big, small?
NORMAN	No, no, more sort of in between, but very nice, very homely.
ROSE	Homely?

NORMAN   Very good in the kitchen, with cooking and
            bottling fruit. Very good in amateur theatricals and
            does a lot for the church.

KURT   Sounds like the average wife. Good to have around
            the house.

NORMAN   Oh yes, very good around the house. Not a speck
            of dust anywhere.

ROSE   What's she like in bed?

NORMAN   (*after a pause*) Very understanding.

            (SVEN *enters with two bottles of Schnapps. He is
            also wearing a pudding bowl shaped hat, made of
            red leather, with a horn on either side of it.*)

SVEN   The Schnapps! The "Iron Man's" drink, and the
            hat I am winning in the contest.

ROSE   Very fetching. I like the little horns.

STANLEY   Not ticklish, are you Rose?

ROSE   I don't see you ever being an "Iron Man".

SVEN   Here Stanley, try it on.

            (*He puts it on* STANLEY'S *head.*)

SVEN   There you are! It changes your whole personality.

STANLEY   You mean if I walked into a party in Sweden girls
            would throw themselves at me?

HILDA   More likely to throw themselves out the window.

            (KURT *smacks her bottom.*)

KURT   (*laughing*) I like a woman with a sense of humour.
            That was good joke, yes?

STANLEY   I've heard better.

SVEN   We know the English love to laugh at themselves.

HILDA	Some of them have to.

(STANLEY *removes his hat*.)

STANLEY	Thank you, Sven. I think it suits you better.

(KURT *is pouring out the Schnapps*.)

KURT	Come now, it's time for a drink before we finally settle the deal.
NORMAN	I thought we had settled. You've had the contracts for weeks.
HILDA	Contracts for what?
STANLEY	We're selling our company to Kurt and Sven.
HILDA	What sort of company would that be?
STANLEY	Haulage.
HILDA	Haulage. Sounds fascinating, doesn't it, Rose?
ROSE	Yes, all those big lorry drivers with hairy arms. They look so strong, almost Godlike, sitting up there in their cabs, and giving you a nice wink as they pull off.
NORMAN	They don't do that to you I hope.
ROSE	Sometimes.
KURT	It's a small outfit in Huddersfield, Bigley and Harris.
HILDA	Not the Bigley and Harris?
KURT	You've heard of them?
HILDA	Very successful. You see their trucks everywhere.
KURT	Do you?
HILDA	Yes.
SVEN	They only have thirty.

HILDA	They must be very busy then because you see them everywhere.

(The men have been given a glass of Schnapps.)

KURT	We drink now to the deal. Bottoms up and no heel taps.
SVEN	Skol.
KURT	Prost.
OTHERS	Cheers.

(They all knock it back in one.)

NORMAN	I should've worn the "Iron Man" hat. That's enough to blow the top of your head off.
SVEN	A few of these and you feel nothing.
NORMAN	Thanks for the warning.
HILDA	You must be getting a fortune, Mr Bigley.
STANLEY	No more that it's worth, a fair price. Eighty thousand a truck.
SVEN	We were thinking of a figure a little less than that.
ROSE	Have another drink, "Iron Man".

(ROSE fills his glass.)

KURT	Fill the others, Hildegard.

(KURT gives her the other bottle.)

KURT	Give one to Stanley.
HILDA	Come along, Mr Bigley, get in the mood.

(STANLEY puts a hand over the glass.)

STANLEY	No thanks, love.
HILDA	I insist!

(HILDA *then shows him that she's putting her thumb over the top of the bottle.*)

STANLEY   Oh, all right then, fill it up.

HILDA   Let me see you down it in one.

(STANLEY *pretends to drink and does a little stagger.*)

STANLEY   It's good stuff is that.

KURT   Rose, do the honours for my friend Norman.

HILDA   (*hastily*) Let me do it.

ROSE   It's quite all right, Hildegard, I know what I'm doing.

HILDA   He just needs a "thumbful," if you know what I mean.

ROSE   I'm not daft.

(SVEN *takes the bottle from* ROSE.)

SVEN   Here, allow me.

(SVEN *pours a generous drink for* NORMAN *and himself.*)

SVEN   Skol!

NORMAN   Skol.

(*They drink.*)

NORMAN   Phew!

(NORMAN *holds his head.*)

NORMAN   Skull.

STANLEY   Are you all right, Norman?

NORMAN   I think I'm feeling fine. Better than usual.

SVEN   We shall make an "Iron Man" of you yet.

NORMAN   I think I could cope with the swimming and the
                running but I'm not sure about "biding a ricycle."

KURT   What's he talking about?

HILDA   I think the sooner he gets some hot food inside
                him the better.

SVEN   So shall we settle for sixty thousand per truck and
                then we can eat, drink and be naughty.

STANLEY   I'm sorry I can't accept that figure. We settled on
                eighty. It's eighty.

SVEN   Sixty.

KURT   Sixty.

STANLEY   Eighty! Norman? Tell him what we want.

                (NORMAN *holds out his glass*.)

NORMAN   Same again.

                (STANLEY *whips* NORMAN'S *glass away*.)

STANLEY   He means eighty. Don't you?

NORMAN   Do I?

STANLEY   'Course you do.

SVEN   I'm sure you could be persuaded to take a little
                less.

                (NORMAN *picks up a glass*.)

NORMAN   All right. Make it a half.

                (STANLEY *takes* NORMAN'S *glass*.)

STANLEY   Concentrate. We're talking numbers here.

NORMAN   I've only had two.

(*The doorbell rings.*)

NORMAN   Ah ha! That'll be the grub. Excuse me.

             (*He goes to the door.*)

STANLEY   Don't forget to tip the waiter.

NORMAN   (*pompously*) As if I would. I shall give him a coin
             of the realm, and if I'm feeling very generous he
             might get a crisp fiver.

             (*He exits to the door.*)

KURT   I think your Mr Harris is an unknown quantity.

STANLEY   I suspect he's drunk an unknown quantity.

HILDA   He'll be sorry when he gets home.

ROSE   He certainly will.

             (NORMAN *reappears.*)

NORMAN   Stanley? Prepare yourself.

STANLEY   Does it look tasty?

NORMAN   Very.

STANLEY   Enough for everybody?

NORMAN   More than enough! It's Sabrina and Valerie.

HILDA
ROSE   }   Sabrina and Valerie?
STANLEY

             (SABRINA *and* VALERIE *enter. They are both big
             girls.* SABRINA *is English and* VALERIE *is
             Australian. They give the men a cheerful wave.*)

SABRINA }   Hello boys!
VALERIE

             (*Curtain.*)

ACT TWO

The same. The action is continuous.

SABRINA   Evening all. I should explain we've had a bit of a
           cock-up.

NORMAN   Oh really?

SABRINA   When we got to the punter's apartment he'd OD'd
           on Viagra and he's in intensive care. And so I said
           to my friend Valerie, as we're up for it anyway,
           let's nip round to the hotel and see if the two
           gentlemen need some company.

HILDA   The two gentlemen are already suited, thank you.

SABRINA   All right ducks, don't get your knickers in a twist,
           that's if you're wearing any.

ROSE   Watch your language please. There are men
           present.

KURT   Don't mind us. We like a little spice in the
           conversation.

SABRINA   Which of you naughty boys requested two ladies?

NORMAN }   He did.
STANLEY }

SABRINA   On the docket it says Mr Harris.

NORMAN   That's me.

ROSE   He's married. He's changed his mind.

VALERIE   They all say that. But we'll soon change it back
           again.

NORMAN   Yes.

ROSE   Unhand him, please.

VALERIE   Is he yours?

SVEN   No, this lady is with me.

             (KURT *pats* HILDA'S *bottom*.)

KURT   And this is mine.

VALERIE   Then it would seem to me that you're two girls short.

KURT   Why didn't you say that you had ordered two more, Stanley?

STANLEY   We didn't. We only ordered two, but we were told they were cancelled.

HILDA   That'll be when you ordered us.

STANLEY   That's right, yes.

ROSE   And by chance we just happened to be in the area.

SABRINA   Work the hotels do you?

ROSE   Oh yes.

VALERIE   Not easy, getting up to the room without being spotted.

ROSE   We haven't had that trouble, have we Hildegard?

HILDA   No. But then they don't tend to stop the more sophisticated woman.

ROSE   I dare say you were questioned, were you?

SABRINA   Oh yeah. But we said we had an appointment with Mr Harris.

VALERIE   Sorry I'm late, Mr Harris, but I'll give you extra time.

NORMAN   Oh, ta.

STANLEY   (*chuckling*) That'll be for injury no doubt.

SABRINA   What's your name, Cheeky?

STANLEY   (*primly*) I'm Mr Bigley.

SABRINA   That's a bit forward. What's your first name?

STANLEY   Stanley.

SABRINA   Well Stan, I'm Sabrina, so it looks like you're mine for the night.

HILDA   Let's not be hasty. I mean, who goes with who isn't set in stone. I've had my eye on Stanley ever since he walked in.

KURT   Oh Hildegard, you are playing hard to get. I like that.

            (KURT *holds* HILDA, *with his hands on her bottom*.)

HILDA   Not yet, Kurt. And not there, either.

            (HILDA *moves* KURT's *hand away*.)

VALERIE   Which way's the bathroom?

KURT   One in there. Use mine.

SABRINA   I'll come with you. I've done me tights in.

            (SABRINA *and* VALERIE *exit together, to bedroom R.*)

SVEN   It looks like we're going to have quite a party.

KURT   Well, Mr Harris, I think you are going to have a hot tropical night.

NORMAN   I think she'd be quite a handful, don't you?

ROSE   Too much for you.

NORMAN   You're probably right.

KURT   You English. I can't understand how you won the war. What about some Dunkirk spirit?

STANLEY	(*raising glass*) No, I'm all right with this, thank you.

HILDA	It's not a question of courage, it's just that some men like the more motherly type, they need their confidence building.

STANLEY	That's very true.

KURT	I can't see you having any problem with Sabrina. She looks like the wildest piece of rumpo I've ever seen . . .

STANLEY	Right up my street! If I wasn't married . . .

KURT	This could be a terrible waste. She looks like she would enjoy handling a real man.

SVEN	Perhaps an "Iron Man"?

KURT	No, Sven, for once I was thinking of myself.

SVEN	You could borrow my hat.

KURT	I don't want to look like a complete stumble-bum.

SVEN	You said you liked my hat.

KURT	On you it looks good. But I think the hat might cramp my style. This Sabrina is an Amazon of Wagnerian proportions. Wunderbar.

HILDA	(*piqued*) Looks dead common, if you ask me. I'm surprised a distinguished man like yourself could be taken in by such a piece of rough.

STANLEY	She looked all right to me.

NORMAN	And me.

ROSE	Nobody asked for your opinion.

HILDA	You see Kurt, you being a foreigner, your ear can't pick out the subtleties of our accents. You see Rose and I speak what is known as 'Standard BBC English.' But Sabrina is, frankly, very low class.

KURT   She hasn't come here to talk.

NORMAN   She's come to party.

HILDA   Not with you, Norman.

KURT   Don't be so bossy. You're a very bossy woman.

HILDA   I am not!

STANLEY   You are.

           (HILDA *rounds on him.*)

HILDA   You what?

STANLEY   I mean, first impressions do indicate a certain
           brusqueness. I'd try and curb it if I were you, or
           we won't book you again.

HILDA   Just wait 'til I get my hands on you . . .

KURT   Ah, now we see how to get her excited. Threaten
           her with redundancy and suddenly she's keen for
           action.

SVEN   Before we get stuck in, can we establish that
           you're paying for those girls, as well as these?

HILDA   No they're not!

KURT   You have a very dominant personality.

SVEN   Maybe she is into domination.

KURT   Is that what you're famous for?

ROSE   No, actually, it's her Yorkshire pudding she's
           famous for.

KURT   It's what?

ROSE   Yorkshire pudding. Nobody can make them rise
           like she can.

SVEN	Fascinating, but I still want to know who's paying for these extra girls.
STANLEY	I can't see it's down to us.
KURT	Sven, let's you and I go and negotiate with Sabrina and Valerie.
SVEN	Excuse us, will you?
STANLEY	Certainly, be my guest.
KURT	We are your guests, remember?
SVEN	I wonder if Sabrina and Valerie can do the Yorkshire pudding?
ROSE	I doubt it. Takes years of practice. Mine always go flat half way through.
SVEN	I think we won't try the Yorkshire pudding.
	(KURT *and* SVEN *exit.*)
HILDA	Well, this is a pretty kettle of fish. (*To* STANLEY.) I blame you.
STANLEY	Me?
HILDA	You should've shut the door on them.
STANLEY	I should have shut the door on you.
HILDA	Well, that's rich, that is, we're having to save your bacon, while I'm being mauled by a man with more hands than an octopus.
STANLEY	Don't give me that. You were leading him on.
HILDA	I was not! I can't help it if I have chemical pheromones that excite his libido.
STANLEY	I've never noticed them.

HILDA   You can't see them, it's an aura. It's in nature –
                 it's what attracted you to me when we first met –
                 pheromones.

STANLEY   Fiddlesticks . . . What attracted me to you was
                 your tight little cycling shorts as you pedalled up
                 Hinchcliff Hill.

HILDA   I never saw you.

STANLEY   I was in the Morris Minor behind you. I was so
                 near, I could read the maker's name.

HILDA   Raleigh?

STANLEY   No, Marks and Spencer.

ROSE   Never mind the ferry-mones, what are we going to
                 do about those two terrible girls?

NORMAN   They're not terrible, they're very nice.

ROSE   If you were sober, you wouldn't think that. I'm not
                 casting disparagements, but did you see the
                 shoes?

HILDA   Oh, I know!

ROSE   Minnie Mouse platforms have never been
                 fashionable.

NORMAN   (*chuckling*) You won't have to worry, they'll be
                 coming off soon.

ROSE   I don't know what's got into Norman.

STANLEY   Half a pint of Schnapps, if you must know. Now
                 Norman, pull yourself together, you're an
                 accountant, you're the one who's got to have the
                 figures at his fingertips.

NORMAN   I'm perfectly capable of handling figures. It's not
                 difficult to sell eighty trucks for thirty thousand
                 each is it?

STANLEY	No. Any mug could do that. What's more difficult is to sell thirty trucks for eighty thousand each.
NORMAN	Who's doing that?
STANLEY	We are! Or we were until you took over the lead in "Lost Weekend".
ROSE	Ray Milland, wasn't it?
HILDA	Yes, he went bald early, didn't he?
STANLEY	We'll all be going bald, if we don't get this damn contract signed.
ROSE	You already are.
HILDA	Don't blame us, you're the brains, we're just here as company.
STANLEY	There seems to be a surplus of that.
NORMAN	Why don't you two slip off now, you might just catch the 10.18.
ROSE	What and leave you here, with those two call-girls?
NORMAN	They're not for us.
ROSE	Your name's on the docket.
STANLEY	No, but they're paying for those girls out of their own pocket. It's nothing to do with us.
HILDA	Suppose you get invited to join in for an orgy?
NORMAN	Well, that's different.
ROSE	That's what I thought. So you can forget about the 10.18. (*To* HILDA.) You can see how easy Norman could be led astray.
HILDA	Stanley wouldn't be far behind him, I can tell you.

STANLEY   Oh ye of little faith. The boot's on the other foot.
            How d'you think Norman and I felt seeing you two
            having your bottoms pinched by those two men?

HILDA   It was all in the line of duty.

ROSE   They don't seem in a hurry to get down to
            business.

HILDA   I don't wish to brag, but Kurt was. What he
            whispered in my ear wasn't sweet nothings.

ROSE   I meant the contract, Hilda.

STANLEY   There's always a psychological moment when you
            know they're ready to sign. Let's hope those girls
            don't wear them out. At least you two are safe,
            you'll be with us, so you won't have to suffer the
            indignity of having your bums pinched. Not by
            them anyway!

HILDA   What do you mean by that?

STANLEY   Norman and I might have to, just for the sake of
            appearances. Don't forget you're supposed to be
            on the game.

ROSE   How did I start off as an elegant dinner
            companion, and suddenly end up on the game?

NORMAN   You're only pretending.

STANLEY   What I'm saying is, you mustn't get upset if we
            start getting frisky with you.

HILDA   Upset? It'll be quite a pleasant change, won't it,
            Rose?

ROSE   Well Norman's never been the frisky type.

STANLEY   Well he better be tonight.

NORMAN   Have we decided who's with who?

STANLEY   I beg your pardon?

NORMAN   Well, we could make it look more realistic, if we
           swap about a bit.

ROSE   How do you make that out?

NORMAN   The trouble is, whenever I try to get frisky with
           you, you always laugh.

ROSE   I can't help it. He pulls such funny faces.

NORMAN   I think I could be frisky with Hilda.

HILDA   You're a bit of a dark horse.

ROSE   In that case, you won't mind if I allow Stanley a
           little leeway?

NORMAN   No, fair do's. Come on Hilda, sit on my knee.

STANLEY   You're in a bit of a hurry, aren't you?

NORMAN   We've got to get a bit of practice in. Rose, you do
           the same with Stanley.

           (HILDA *sits on* NORMAN'S *knee*.)

NORMAN   How's that? Are you comfy?

HILDA   If you could just move your car keys, I'll be fine.

NORMAN   They're in my overcoat.

HILDA   (*puzzled*) Oh.

           (ROSE *is sitting on* STANLEY'S *lap*.)

ROSE   Come on, Stanley, look as though you fancy me.

STANLEY   I am doing. I am giving you my come-to-bed-eyes
           look.

ROSE   Oh.

           (ROSE *stares into his eyes*.)

ROSE   Are you thinking of sex?

STANLEY   Why?

ROSE   Your pupils are getting very big.

STANLEY   That's because you've cut off the blood supply of this leg.

ROSE   Sorry. I'll get on both of them. Hang on while I get comfy. (ROSE *wiggles*.) Is that better?

STANLEY   It's getting that way.

(KURT *and* SABRINA *enter*.)

SABRINA   We've done the business.

STANLEY   Oh good. Are you ready to sign, Kurt?

KURT   Later. We've just been settling on the price.

STANLEY   Satisfactory I trust.

KURT   London is getting very expensive.

SABRINA   But we'll make it worth it. And we always charge more for an orgy.

HILDA   Orgy?

ROSE   We don't do those. We're more your elegant dining companions.

SABRINA   Why don't you pack these women off home? I reckon they're amateurs.

HILDA }
ROSE }   Amateurs!

SABRINA   If I were you, I'd try and flog it in King's Cross.

HILDA   How dare you!

KURT   Please don't be so rude to these charming ladies.

HILDA   Thank you, Kurt.

KURT   If we're all going to spend some time together, we
        want to be friendly – in some cases, very friendly.

        (*The doorbell rings.*)

STANLEY   Will you get it, Norman?

HILDA   Get it yourself. Norman's quite comfy where he is.

        (STANLEY *gets up.*)

STANLEY   Excuse me, Rose.

ROSE   You haven't ordered more ladies have you?

STANLEY   Don't be ridiculous.

NORMAN   I hope it's my supper. My stomach's rumbling.

HILDA   Is that what it was? I thought something was up
        down there.

STANLEY   (*off*) Thank you, I can manage. No! Don't come in!
        I said no! I'm in a meeting.

        (STANLEY *appears with a food trolley, which has
        side flaps. It is laden with food. The flaps stay
        down throughout.*)

KURT   Ah, at last! (*To* SABRINA.) Go and fetch the others.

SABRINA   Looks good. I'm starving, haven't had a chance to
        eat. I've been off my feet all afternoon. (*Exits.*)

KURT   I don't want to seem ungrateful, Stanley, but
        although these girls are sexy to look at, they don't
        have the class of these two.

STANLEY   I have to agree.

HILDA   Yes, he does.

KURT   So, as we are the guests we will have first choice,
        and you and Norman can have first go at the
        bimbos.

STANLEY   Let's not rush into anything. After you've had some food and a few drinks you might feel differently.

KURT   Why should I?

HILDA   You can tell he's a gentleman, he's got taste.

KURT   You're just the type of charming companions one could introduce anywhere. I have a yacht trip planned in April from Rome to Capri and then on to the Greek Islands. Would you be interested? It's only two weeks.

HILDA   But aren't you happily married?

KURT   No. I'm happily divorced.

HILDA   Can I bring my friend Rose?

KURT   That's up to Sven, it's his yacht.

HILDA   Sounds tempting doesn't it?

ROSE   April? Well, I'll have a look in my diary and see what my bookings are. Capri, that's where Gracie Fields lived. My mother had all her records. She was buried there.

STANLEY   Your mother?

ROSE   No, Gracie Fields.

(SVEN *and* VALERIE *enter.* SVEN *is doing his shirt up.* VALERIE *is now in a short skirt, leopard skin boots, bare midriff and a halter top.*)

ROSE   What have you been up to, Sven?

SVEN   I have a stiff neck, Valerie gave it a little massage.

ROSE   You could have asked me.

VALERIE   You'll have your chance later, petal.

STANLEY   There's a stack of food here. Help yourselves!

(*They all do so.*)

KURT   I see the grapes are there, Hildegard. Don't forget you're going to feed them to me.

(STANLEY *takes a bunch.*)

STANLEY   If there are any left.

SABRINA   (*to* VALERIE) Not often we get fed as well.

VALERIE   If there's any left we'll ask for a doggy bag.

SVEN   Let us all drink a toast. Everyone has a drink, yes?

ROSE   Yes.

SABRINA   Aren't you going to give me one?

KURT   Yes. But have a drink first!

VALERIE   Have you got any champagne?

STANLEY   We're keeping that 'til later, to celebrate our business deal.

VALERIE   Do the deal now, then we can have some bubbly.

STANLEY   Good idea. How about it Kurt?

KURT   If you agree to drop twenty percent, we'll sign now.

STANLEY   No chance.

KURT   No bubbly.

VALERIE   Don't be stingy. What is twenty percent between friends?

NORMAN   About three hundred thousand pounds.

SABRINA   Blimey, you're talking big money. (*To* VALERIE.) I think we've undercharged.

VALERIE   Here, you're not drug dealers, are you?

KURT   Certainly not.

HILDA   Do they look like drug dealers?

VALERIE   He could be.

           (VALERIE *points at* NORMAN.)

ROSE   He's just had a drink, that's all. They're in
           trucking, haulage.

NORMAN   We're selling, they're buying.

SVEN   A toast! I give you a toast from Scandinavia.
           "Deen Skol. Meen Skol alla Vacca Skol!"

SABRINA   Sounds a bit rude.

SVEN   I says, "Your health, my health, all the pretty girls'
           health!"

           (*They all take a sip.*)

VALERIE   Wow! A couple of those would blow my bra off.

NORMAN   Give her another one quickly.

SABRINA   Into the gob, round the gums, look out stomach,
           here it comes . . .

           (*They drink.*)

ROSE   I don't think I have the head for snaps.

KURT   It's Schnapps.

ROSE   Ish it?

HILDA   It's more like French polish. It must be an acquired
           taste.

KURT   And I shall help you to acquire it.

HILDA   Are you trying to lead a girl astray?

KURT   Yes. Are you beginning to feel naughty?

HILDA   I'm certainly not feeling myself.

KURT   Maybe you should lie down for a bit.

HILDA   Just for a bit maybe.

             (KURT *lifts her up and carries her towards the
             bedroom.*)

KURT   Stanley, bring the grapes.

STANLEY   If you don't mind, I'd rather not.

HILDA   Do as you're told!!

             (KURT *carries* HILDA *off, followed by* STANLEY *with
             the grapes.*)

SABRINA   I can see now how she operates. She's very
             professional, isn't she?

VALERIE   Yes, you can always pick up a tip or two from the
             older ones.

SABRINA   Right. Who's turn next?

NORMAN   I'm easy.

ROSE   So am I.

SVEN   Then allow me. Eeny meeny miny . . . mo, which of
             the ladies has to go?

             (SVEN *finishes up pointing at* VALERIE.)

SVEN   Eeny meeny miny . . . mo, which of the ladies has
             to go?

             (SVEN *finishes up on* SABRINA, *so he picks up*
             ROSE.)

SVEN   I will see you later.

             (*As* ROSE *exits in* SVEN'S *arms, she bursts into
             song.*)

ROSE   "Wish me luck as you wave me goodbye . . ."

SABRINA   How did she manage that?

VALERIE	I don't know, he was really tasty.

(STANLEY *enters*.)

STANLEY	I've just seen a side of Hilda I've never seen before.
NORMAN	Stripped off already has she?
STANLEY	Where's Rose?
NORMAN	Tarzan's just carried her off.
VALERIE	Well, you lucky boys, you're left with the real thing.
NORMAN	Yes, I suppose we are.
SABRINA	How does it feel to have a couple of young nymphets about to jump on you?
STANLEY	The first word that comes to mind is apprehensive.
SABRINA	I promise you it's something you won't get at home with the wife.
NORMAN	How did you know we were married?
SABRINA	You can always tell. You've got that henpecked look.
STANLEY	I can assure you Miss . . .
SABRINA	Sabrina.
STANLEY	Sabrina, we are both very happily married men, aren't we, Norman?
NORMAN	After a few years you forget how happy you are.
SABRINA	Then why send for us?
VALERIE	They were feeling frustrated. They wanted to move into fresh pastures, where the grass is greener.

(VALERIE *puts an arm around* NORMAN.)

VALERIE	Have you ever been down . . . under?

NORMAN   No, this is as near as I've got.

STANLEY   The point is, we booked you, not for ourselves,
            but to entertain our business associates. They're
            both very high fliers, and they expect this sort of
            thing, and when you cancelled we had to find two
            more, but since you've turned up we're somewhat
            oversubscribed.

SABRINA   So what do you want then?

STANLEY   If you're not pushed for time, we could have a
            little chat and avail ourselves of this repast.

SABRINA   Oh, all right, make a nice change. What d'you
            want to talk about?

            (*They stand around the food trolley and all help
            themselves.*)

STANLEY   Anything. Er . . . Would you like to kick off, Norman?

NORMAN   Right. What've you been doing today?

STANLEY   Not very tactful, Norman.

SABRINA   I don't discuss my clients.

STANLEY   That's a relief. When you're not busy do you have
            any hobbies?

SABRINA   Oh yeah, I'm taking a Pru Leath cookery course at
            the moment.

STANLEY   Are you?

SABRINA   Very nice class of person there.

VALERIE   She wants me to go too, but I have to stay at home
            as much as possible, for little Duane.

NORMAN   How old is little Duane?

VALERIE   He'll be four in December.

NORMAN   So you are married?

VALERIE	No, it was a love child. It was when the English cricket team came to Sydney for the Test Match.
NORMAN	Four years ago? We lost the series didn't we?
STANLEY	Which side was the father on?
VALERIE	The losing side, but I can't tell you who it was.
STANLEY	No, I quite understand.
VALERIE	But he did drop a vital catch.
NORMAN	A bit clumsy all round then.
VALERIE	(*laughing*) You could say that.
SABRINA	I'm more into soccer. I follow Chelsea, 'cos they've got the best-looking foreigners. Who do you follow?
STANLEY	Norman and I prefer rugby, but the wives aren't that keen.
VALERIE	Well, that's marriage for you, you lose your independence.
NORMAN	Not in our case, we've got no complaints, have we, Stanley?
STANLEY	No, they look after us very well.
SABRINA	How long have you been married?
STANLEY	Nearly twenty years.
SABRINA	Did they marry you for your money?
STANLEY	Good Lord, no. We didn't have any then.
NORMAN	We'd just started our business and we got lucky and it took off. It was hard work to start with because we were driving our own trucks for the first few years, all over the country.
VALERIE	Leaving the wives at home?

NORMAN	Certainly.
VALERIE	How d'you know they weren't having a bit of fun while you were away?
NORMAN	I just know.
STANLEY	You see, with certain women you know you can trust them. They'd never look at another man.

(HILDA *is heard giving an excited yelp, followed by laughter.* STANLEY *is riveted.*)

STANLEY	Er . . . Now where were we?
SABRINA	We were discussing faithful wives.
STANLEY	Oh yes.
VALERIE	I could be faithful, if I was sure I had a faithful man. God fearing, a good Christian. D'you go to church?
NORMAN	Every Sunday.
VALERIE	You would have been my type of man.
NORMAN	Would I?
VALERIE	Oh yes. And I promise you, you would have had a very faithful wife.
NORMAN	Very nice of you to say so. And may I add that I would have counted myself lucky to have found happiness with you and little Duane. But fate has decreed otherwise and I must count my blessings that I have a marriage that's never given me a moment's anxiety.

(ROSE *is heard from the bedroom.*)

ROSE	(*off, laughing*) No Sven, it's your turn to wear the hat.
SABRINA	Those Swedes, they can go on all night you know.
NORMAN	All night?

Sabrina	Well, you get very little daylight up there. It's hardly worth getting out of bed.

(Another scream and excited voices are heard from Rose *and* Sven.)*

Norman   D'you think everything's all right?

Sabrina   So long as he don't pass out before he signs that contract.

Norman   Pass out?

Sabrina   Well it can happen, but it would be a bit of a coincidence, two in one day.

Norman   I think I'll just check.

*(*Norman *starts to go towards the bedroom.* Stanley *holds him back.*)*

Stanley   Don't, Norman, don't. You might upset yourself.

(The bedroom door opens and Rose *appears in the "Iron Man" hat with one horn only.)*

Rose   Excuse me. But have either of you ladies got an aspirin?

Norman   *(whispering to* Stanley*)* Oh, she's got a headache.

Valerie   I've got some here.

Stanley   Correct me if I'm wrong, but didn't that hat have two horns?

Rose   Did it?

Norman   Yes it did.

Rose   You're quite right. I took one off for bad behaviour. Where's that aspirin?

Valerie   Here you are.

NORMAN   Don't forget you'll feel better when you've had a couple of those.

ROSE   It's not for me, it's for Sven.

(ROSE *exits to bedroom*.)

NORMAN   Well, I'll go to the foot of our stairs.

STANLEY   What does she look like in that hat.

(HILDA *enters wearing a towelling dressing gown and turban*.)

HILDA   We need more grapes.

STANLEY   What's with the turban?

HILDA   Well you see, we're playing out fantasies. He's "Anthony" and I'm "Cleopatra", and he's just come all the way from Rome.

VALERIE   Blimey, some fantasy.

STANLEY   The grapes are finished. How d'you fancy prunes and custard?

HILDA   He's not kinky. He'll have to make do with bananas.

STANLEY   Bananas?

SABRINA   Let us know if you need a hand.

HILDA   No, he's quite happy with his little "Cleopatra."

STANLEY   Tell him to keep his hands off your asp.

HILDA   Don't be so vulgar.

(HILDA *exits with bananas, which are in a silver bowl*.)

VALERIE   D'you want some cheese?

STANLEY   No thanks, I've lost my appetite.

(NORMAN *sits on the sofa.* VALERIE *joins him.*)

SABRINA Can't we tempt you with anything?

STANLEY Well, to be honest, I think the answer's yes.

KURT (*off, calling out*) And now we take a trip up the Nile.

(*There is a joyful shriek from* HILDA.)

SABRINA D'you fancy a bit?

STANLEY It had crossed my mind.

NORMAN Stanley, think of your wife.

STANLEY I am.

(SABRINA *gives* STANLEY *a piece of tart.*)

SABRINA Here you are darling. And here's a serviette, you don't want to spoil your shirt.

STANLEY Ta.

(STANLEY *sits in chair.* SABRINA *sits on the chair's arm.*)

STANLEY Any objection if I put an arm round you?

SABRINA Listen Stanley, if you're the kind of bloke I think you are, we don't want to do something you might regret.

STANLEY No, I won't.

SABRINA You'd be throwing away twenty years of faithfulness, for the sake of a moment of physical excitement. And I don't want to be the one responsible for that. You see I know I've got this fatal attraction for men. It's not my fault I'm beautiful or sexy. In fact it can be a disadvantage. You never know if a man's just ogling your bits, or he's got deeper feelings.

STANLEY I think I've got both.

VALERIE	What Sabrina says is very true, you ought to take an example from your friend Norman. He and I are sitting next to each other. I dare say he thinks I'm quite a tasty bit of stuff, but he's not thinking of that, he's thinking of his wife.
NORMAN	Am I? Oh yes! But it's a bit like being in the Garden of Eden, I'm sorely tempted.
VALERIE	Oh Norman, I think you're going to disappoint me.
NORMAN	Oh, no I won't!

(NORMAN *grabs her, as her mobile phone goes*.)

VALERIE	Is that yours or mine?
SABRINA	Yours.
VALERIE	Hold on there, petal.

(VALERIE *answers her mobile phone*.)

VALERIE	Oh hello, Mrs Maclean. No, I'm not in the middle of anything . . . Did he have his hot chocolate? Oh well, you'd better put him on . . . Hello my little angel! No, Mummy can't come just yet, she's with some nice gentleman . . . You want to talk to them? Hold on . . . (*To* NORMAN.) Have a word with little Duane.
NORMAN	I'd rather not . . .
VALERIE	You could tell him a nursery rhyme. You must know some rhymes.
NORMAN	Oh, I know one.

(NORMAN *takes* VALERIE'S *mobile phone*.)

NORMAN	Are you there Duane? Right.

"Little Miss Muffet sat on her tuffet,
Eating her curds and whey!
There came a big spider,

That sat down beside her, and . . . Duane? . . .
Duane? . . . Pull yourself together!

(NORMAN *hands the phone back to* VALERIE.)

NORMAN He's crying his eyes out.

VALERIE (*into phone*) Don't cry, my darling . . . Don't
worry, there's no spider . . . If you promise to go
to sleep I'll sing you a little song. Ready?

"Sweetest little fellow everybody knows,
Don't know what to call him,
But he's mighty like a rose
Looking at his Mammy,
His eyes so shiny blue,
Make you think that heaven,
Is coming close to you."

Duane? . . . Duane?

(VALERIE *turns to* NORMAN, *who is dabbing a tear
away.* VALERIE *switches her phone off and puts it
down.*)

I think that's done it.

NORMAN Where were we before the phone went?

VALERIE We were getting to know each other on a spiritual
level. You were telling me how faithful you were to
your wife.

NORMAN Oh, was I?

VALERIE What's her name?

NORMAN Er . . . er . . . Mrs Harris.

VALERIE Her Christian name.

STANLEY Rosalind.

NORMAN Rosalind.

VALERIE	That's a pretty name. Lucky woman to have a man like you. Maybe one day I'll meet a man like you.

(NORMAN *opens his arms.*)

NORMAN	You already have!
VALERIE	But you're married.
NORMAN	What if I was divorced?
VALERIE	Why are you contemplating divorce, when you're so happily married?
NORMAN	I hadn't thought about it until just now.
VALERIE	You mean, my nice warm body has rekindled something that was previously dormant?
NORMAN	Well . . . Now you mention it . . .
SABRINA	Nothing to be ashamed of. How about you, Stan, you getting it regular?
STANLEY	Well, I er, suppose, yes, more or less.
SABRINA	I'll mark that down as "less."
STANLEY	I don't thing that's anything I want to discuss, it's not relevant.
SABRINA	You sound a bit inhibited to me.
STANLEY	No, you see, after a few satisfying years, it's not so much on your mind, is it Norman?
NORMAN	No. Sometimes, you'd be happy to settle for an egg and bacon.
VALERIE	That's one of the saddest things I've ever heard.
STANLEY	One of the saddest things I've ever heard.
NORMAN	That's just between ourselves.

SABRINA   I think both you boys need your sex life
           revitalising. And although you're reluctant, I'm
           sure Val and I could do you a favour, couldn't we?

           (VALERIE *looks at her watch.*)

VALERIE   Shouldn't take long.

NORMAN   Right, well, that's settled.

VALERIE   That tie looks very formal, why don't you loosen
           it? Here, let me. . .

           (VALERIE *loosens* NORMAN'S *tie.*)

SABRINA   (*to* STANLEY) How about taking your jacket off?

STANLEY   Yes, it is a bit hot.

           (SABRINA *puts her arms round him in removing his
           jacket. Her proximity is exciting him.*)

VALERIE   Now let's undo your shirt.

NORMAN   Steady on, you're tickling.

VALERIE   I think you like a little tickle.

NORMAN   Perhaps.

VALERIE   Let's find out where you like it most.

           (VALERIE *goes for him and* NORMAN *crawls on all
           fours round the back of the sofa.* VALERIE *joins
           him. She is obviously sitting on him, and her head
           and shoulders are visible above the back of the
           sofa.*)

NORMAN   Oh Valerie, no!

VALERIE   When they say no, they mean yes.

           (*They disappear from view.* STANLEY *rises and is
           pushed back into the chair by* SABRINA.)

STANLEY   You're stronger than you look.

SABRINA   You haven't had a look yet.

           (SABRINA *undoes her halter top and reveals a skimpy bra.*)

STANLEY   (*impressed*) Bloody Nora!

SABRINA   What do you think of these?

STANLEY   You don't get many of those to the kilo.

NORMAN   (*hidden behind the sofa*) Help!

VALERIE   You don't need help.

NORMAN   That's my belt, Stanley!

STANLEY   You're on your own. I've got my eyes full.

           (SABRINA *is gyrating gently as she undoes her skirt.* VALERIE *and* NORMAN *are out of sight.*)

SABRINA   As you can gather, I do a bit of lap-dancing.

STANLEY   Do you?

SABRINA   Haven't you been to one of those clubs?

STANLEY   No.

SABRINA   They're very popular.

STANLEY   I can see why.

SABRINA   I'll strip down to my G-string.

STANLEY   Yes, well, all in good time.

           (*The phone in the suite rings.*)

STANLEY   Oh heck! Can you get that, Norman?

           (NORMAN'S *head appears from behind the sofa.*)

NORMAN   I'm slightly incapacitated at the moment.

STANLEY   (*to* SABRINA) Just remember where we got to.

(STANLEY *answers the phone.*)

STANLEY   Yes . . . Yes . . . Oh.

          (*He cups the phone.*)

          It's Mrs Clitheroe for Rose . . .

NORMAN   Tell her she's busy.

STANLEY   She says it's urgent.

          (NORMAN *goes to the bedroom, pulling up his trousers. He knocks on the door.*)

NORMAN   Rose? Your Mam's on the phone.

VALERIE   Is that the Madame?

STANLEY   The Madame, yes.

NORMAN   Rose!

VALERIE   They shouldn't call when you're with a client. Let me have a word with her.

          (VALERIE *goes to take the phone.*)

NORMAN   No!

          (ROSE *enters in a large bath towel.*)

ROSE   What is it?

VALERIE   It's your agency. Another booking.

ROSE   What?

          (NORMAN *winks at* ROSE *and passes her the phone.*)

NORMAN   It's Mrs Clitheroe.

ROSE   Oh. (*Into phone, loudly.*) Yes, it's me, Rose. No I haven't left yet . . . I say, I haven't (*To the others.*) Deaf as a post. (*Into phone.*) I'm still here! We were helping to entertain the clients from abroad . . . Well, if Violet's not well, I'll take her place, but I can't cope with that Big Tom. I did my

back in last time. I'll call you when I get home.
Bye.

(ROSE *puts the phone down.*)

VALERIE How big is this "Big Tom"?

ROSE It's a whopper. It really needs four of us to get it
moving. And if you don't let go in time, you can
find yourself on the ceiling.

SABRINA What d'you charge for that?

ROSE Nothing. It's purely voluntary.

VALERIE You mean freebies?

ROSE Yes. Sunday mornings you can hear it all over
Huddersfield.

(KURT *enters from the bedroom, draped in a sheet,
á la toga, and carrying* HILDA.)

KURT More Schnapps for the "Queen of the Nile".

STANLEY Go easy with her.

HILDA Put me down, "Anthony".

STANLEY Are you all right?

HILDA I'll tell you what, it's bloody hot in Egypt.

(KURT *suddenly sees the half-naked* SABRINA.)

KURT Mein Gott. Could this be my "Nefertitty"?

SABRINA If it's included in the price, yes.

(KURT *leads* SABRINA *to the bedroom.*)

KURT I may be gone for sometime.

(STANLEY *stands blocking his way.*)

STANLEY You may be gone for good. You're not going
anywhere with "Nefertitty" until you agree to our
terms.

KURT   All right. Seventy thousand.

STANLEY   Eighty or the deal's off.

KURT   What the hell. Eighty.

STANLEY   Shake on it.

KURT   Get Sven to agree and we'll sign.

            (KURT *goes towards the bedroom with* SABRINA.)

KURT   I can't wait to see those pyramids by moonlight.

SABRINA   Cheeky.

            (KURT *and* SABRINA *exit.*)

STANLEY   Rose, love, would you nip back in to Sven, tell him
            his partner's agreed the deal if he will, which
            means you've got to get him up ten percent.

ROSE   I don't think I could wear that hat again.

STANLEY   If we doubled your fee, would you do it?

ROSE   It's not that. He's unconscious.

NORMAN   What did you do to him?

ROSE   It's all that Schnapps.

STANLEY   He's got to put his name on the contract. He can't
            do that if he's passed out.

VALERIE   If you care to double my fee, I guarantee I'll have
            him up and about in no time.

            (VALERIE *exits to the other bedroom.*)

NORMAN   If anybody can do it, she can.

ROSE   Oh, and how would you know?

NORMAN.   Well, I mean, she's trained for that sort of thing.
            She told us, didn't she Stanley?

STANLEY   Yes, poor soul, she's a single mother. It can't be
            easy.

NORMAN	Not with little Duane to cope with. He's quite a handful.
HILDA	Trying to get more money out of you, I dare say. Just a sob story. Typical.
NORMAN	Oh no, I've spoken to him.
HILDA	How?
NORMAN	The baby-sitter called, saying she couldn't get him to sleep.
STANLEY	So Norman told him a story about a big spider and gave the poor little bugger nightmares.
ROSE	I've never heard such a load of rubbish in my life.
NORMAN	It's the truth.
ROSE	So why did you take your trousers off to tell him?
STANLEY	They were already off.
ROSE	How could you?
STANLEY	I don't know what you two have been up to, but we've been fighting a rearguard action here. They were paid to entertain, and being professionals they didn't want to disappoint.
NORMAN	You see, they take pride in their occupation.
STANLEY	As I'm sure you've been doing in yours.
HILDA	How dare you?
STANLEY	Albeit of a temporary nature.
HILDA	I can't speak for Rose, but I've been fighting for my honour in that room.
ROSE	It wasn't easy for me. And he fully deserved that "Iron Man" hat.

(*The phone rings in the suite.* STANLEY *picks it up and hands it to* ROSE.)

STANLEY   Be your mother again.

ROSE   Hello? Oh yes . . . (*To the others.*) It's only the hall porter. (*Into phone.*) Sorry? . . . The police want Mr Bigley and Mr Harris? . . . How does that affect us? . . . A burst water main . . . Range Rover, yes . . . Oh no . . . (*To the others.*) They've got to dig the road up, so the police are going to remove it, if you don't get down with the keys.

STANLEY   Oh God. Come on Norman, let's sort it out.

NORMAN   Where's my belt?

(ROSE *picks up* NORMAN'S *belt.*)

ROSE   Would this be it?

NORMAN   Oh, ta. Who's got the keys?

(NORMAN *takes the belt and starts threading it through the loops.*)

STANLEY   In my overcoat.

(STANLEY *takes them from the coat.*)

HILDA   You don't both have to go.

STANLEY   We may have to push it.

NORMAN   There's not a lot left in the battery.

ROSE   Have you any left in yours?

NORMAN   You watch your tongue, woman.

(STANLEY *and* NORMAN *exit through the hall.*)

ROSE   I have never been spoken to like that. I don't know what's come over him.

HILDA   Stanley sounded a bit off-hand, considering what we've been through.

ROSE   Oh, I know.

        (*They sit on the sofa.*)

HILDA   They're different, aren't they, continentals?

ROSE   Oh, chalk and cheese.

HILDA   But considerate.

ROSE   Was he passionate?

HILDA   Yes, but in a very nice way. I felt I was being
        wooed.

ROSE   (*chuckling*) I was being quite wooed with Sven.

HILDA   Now then, Rose, that's not like you.

ROSE   What about Kurt? Was he romantic?

HILDA   Oh yes! He took off his Y-fronts, they were red,
        and wrapped them round the bedside lamp. The
        atmosphere in that room changed totally. You
        don't realise how important lighting can be.
        Everything looks so different.

ROSE   Well, it would be darker for a start.

HILDA   Oh, it was.

ROSE   But you could still see everything?

HILDA   Oh, very clearly. You see Stanley, bless him,
        would never have thought of something like that.

ROSE   No, Norman's the same. We've only got dimmer
        switches.

HILDA   How did Sven's imagination manifest itself?

ROSE   Well, it was a bit like an assault course. And when
        it comes to underwear he's very quick.

HILDA   With his or yours?

ROSE   Mine of course. I didn't see when he took his off.
            He came out of the bathroom just like the day he
            was born.

HILDA   What crawling?

ROSE   No, starkers. Of course he had his hat on.

HILDA   Oh, he's got some manners then?

ROSE   Oh yes.

HILDA   Go on.

ROSE   Then a remarkable thing happened. I felt a hand
            behind my back and before I knew it, my corset
            was on the floor.

HILDA   No!

ROSE   (*dropping towel*) Yes, and he was very
            complimentary. It's nice when they notice, isn't it!

HILDA   Yes, Kurt noticed a little mole. I'd forgotten all
            about it, it's just in the small of my back, quite low
            down. Round about there . . .

            (HILDA *removes her bathrobe*.)

ROSE   Oh yes, I see.

            (*They are both now un-selfconsciously in their
            basques*.)

HILDA   He gave it a kiss. Kurt was very demonstrative. He
            likes to start off slowly, and he did something with
            a grape that I didn't think was feasible.

ROSE   The mind boggles.

HILDA   I got the giggles.

ROSE   We are not supposed to giggle. We're hookers.

HILDA   I keep forgetting, I'm having such a good time.

ROSE   So am I.

(VALERIE *enters.*)

VALERIE   Well, that's a job well done. I managed to revive him and he's agreed to the extra ten percent.

ROSE   How did you manage to persuade him?

VALERIE   One of the tricks of the trade. Have you noticed that there's always a point when a man can't say "No"?

ROSE   You're so right.

HILDA   What about those two businessmen from the North?

ROSE   Oh yes, what were their names?

HILDA   Stanley was it?

VALERIE   And Stormin' Norman.

ROSE   Stormin'?

VALERIE   Not to start with. You see he was suffering from a lot of inhibitions. It appears that he's been married for at least twenty years to the same woman.

ROSE   What's that got to do with it?

VALERIE   They get bored, they forget the romance.

ROSE   It happens to a lot of men.

VALERIE   I'm talking about the wives. Norman tells me his woman goes to bed in curlers.

HILDA   Well, I never . . .

VALERIE   Who wants to go to bed with a radio transmitter?

ROSE   Perhaps her hair is fine and soft and she was hoping to make her hair look nice for the next day.

VALERIE   No point in that. He'll be at work. Night time is sex time for married people. For us it's twenty-four hours a day.

HILDA	I don't know how we cope.
VALERIE	At least we get job satisfaction. You should have seen the look on Norman's little face.
ROSE	When?
VALERIE	When I had him pinned behind the sofa, telling him what I had in mind for him.
ROSE	I can imagine.

(SABRINA *enters with her hair in two rough plaits.*)

KURT	(*off*) Come back. (KURT *sings a snatch of Wagner, still off.* SABRINA *shuts the door.*)
SABRINA	I take my hat off to you, Hildergard. Talk about sex drive, he should have his licence endorsed.
HILDA	Still going strong, was he?
SABRINA	Was he ever.
HILDA	Still "Mark Anthony?"
SABRINA	No. We left Egypt and went into opera. He plaited my hair, gave me a loo brush and told me I was "Brunhilde" in something by Wagner.
VALERIE	And what was he, petal?
SABRINA	He put the fruit bowl on his head and said he was "Siegfried" and going to do the "Ring."
VALERIE	I hope you charged extra for singing.
ROSE	(*to* HILDA) I think you got off rather lightly.
HILDA	(*to* SABRINA) And all that on top of entertaining that other gentleman – er – Stanley, wasn't it?
SABRINA	Oh him. He was hard work. I did some of my best moves for him. I undulated right in front of his nose and nothing, not a twitch.

HILDA   Some men have terrific will power. Particularly if they're happily married.

SABRINA It's not will power. I've seen it before. It's a sign they've got a bossy wife and they even look at another woman . . . they get a right rollocking. Now let's say for argument's sake we was all happily married, instead of being on the game, a bit on the side wouldn't bother us, would it Hildegard?

HILDA   Not if we enjoyed it.

SABRINA And we wouldn't mention it to our husbands.

ROSE   There'd be no point in upsetting them.

VALERIE I think we have the best of all worlds. We can have it when we want it.

         (KURT *enters dramatically singing, with the upturned silver fruit bowl on his head and wearing a dressing gown.*)

HILDA   What do you look like?

KURT   We're only half way through the opera.

HILDA   That's why we're having an interval.

ROSE   Your friend Sven has agreed to the full price for those trucks.

KURT   Oh, well, someone must have made him very happy.

ROSE   It was a combined effort, wasn't it Valerie?

KURT   Oh, a threesome.

VALERIE Yes.

ROSE   I got him going and she finished him off.

KURT   Gott in Himmel, I must get the details.

(KURT *goes hurriedly towards* SVEN'S *room.*)

KURT   When I come back, we'll have a foursome.

VALERIE   Will that be with Sven and two of us, or you and three of us?

KURT   I'll take all four.

(KURT *exits, shutting the door.*)

HILDA   Trouble with him, is that his eyes are bigger than his whatnot.

SABRINA   Listen, as long as they pay we're all game, aren't we?

VALERIE   Count me in. I charge an extra hundred for an orgy. How about you, Hildegard?

HILDA   Er . . . no. We don't do those any more. They can so easily get out of hand.

VALERIE   What about when four of you are pulling that "Big Tom"?

HILDA   Pardon?

ROSE   I was telling them about my Sunday job.

HILDA   Sunday?

ROSE   The one I do for the vicar, you know.

HILDA   (*lost*) Not the Reverend Smollet?

ROSE   You know.

(ROSE *tries to demonstrate by miming pulling up and down on a long rope.*)

SABRINA   Blimey, no wonder you call him "Big Tom."

(STANLEY *and* NORMAN *enter.*)

STANLEY   You wouldn't credit the trouble we've had. The battery was flat. We had to push it to a garage.

NORMAN   They're putting another one in, but they rob you blind in London.

HILDA   One way and another, it's turning out quite an expensive night for you.

STANLEY   How's that?

VALERIE   You promised to double my fee, if I got Sven to raise his sights on the price.

STANLEY   And did he?

VALERIE   He did.

NORMAN   Smashing. Well done.

VALERIE   I can't take all the credit. You can give some to Rose, she really got him going.

STANLEY   Good for you, Rose. What d'you reckon it'll come to?

          (STANLEY *takes a wad of fifty pounds out of his pocket.*)

VALERIE   Call it three hundred and I'll take care of Rose.

SABRINA   But don't mention it to your agency.

ROSE   I wouldn't dream of it.

HILDA   Come along, fair do's. Who was it that got Kurt up in the first place?

STANLEY   I beg your pardon?

HILDA   Financially speaking, I've been socialising above and well beyond the call of duty.

          (STANLEY *and* NORMAN *suddenly become aware that their wives are just wearing basques, and are indistinguishable from the "Escort Girls".*)

STANLEY   Do you know what you look like?

NORMAN   (*nudging him*) Of course they do.

STANLEY   Oh yes. I must say Rose polishes up very well.

NORMAN   (*proudly*) Yes, doesn't she!

ROSE   Nice to get a compliment.

NORMAN   I can certainly see what you saw in Hilda.

STANLEY   I wouldn't mind, but everyone can see it.

HILDA   Feast your eyes, before I put it away.

(HILDA *puts her dressing gown back on.*)

SABRINA   I wish I had your confidence, or have you already made enough to retire?

HILDA   Funny you should say that. We're hoping to, aren't we, Rose?

ROSE   Yes, we've put a deposit down on a couple of little apartments in Marbella.

(ROSE *replaces her towel.*)

SABRINA   You deserve it. You've been at it a long time, I suppose?

ROSE   When did we start?

HILDA   About twenty years ago.

VALERIE   It must be great, being able to put up your feet for free.

(KURT *appears in the bedroom door with* SVEN.)

SVEN   My head. Now before I sign the contract, is there any of you ladies I've missed out on?

SABRINA   Me and Hildegard.

STANLEY   Save them 'til later. Get this contract signed first.

HILDA   Save me for later? You make me sound like an "After Eight".

STANLEY   No offence. Norman, get the contracts out.

(NORMAN *goes to his briefcase.*)

NORMAN	We'll need witnesses. Shall I call on the manager?

(STANLEY *indicates the women.*)

STANLEY	Not unless you want to give him a heart attack.
NORMAN	We're a bit stuck then.
KURT	How can you say that? We have four witnesses.
STANLEY	But what about where it says "Occupation"? You can't put down tarts.
HILDA	How dare you. We're escorts.
ROSE	High class.
STANLEY	High class or not, you and your friend here cannot sign your names.
SVEN	I always find these girls have other jobs. You know, waitresses . . . veterinary surgeons . . .
KURT	Hildegard, have you any other occupation?
HILDA	No. Rose and myself are full time.
VALERIE	This one even does it on Sundays. But speaking for myself I'm a qualified aerobics teacher.
STANLEY	That's a surprise.
NORMAN	(*smiling*) Not to me. But that'll do nicely.
KURT	What about our lovely Sabrina?
SABRINA	Put me down as, "receptionist".
HILDA	Where do you do that?
SABRINA	At the agency, when they're short handed.
VALERIE	Which is quite often.
STANLEY	Right. Let's get on with it.

ACT TWO

(STANLEY *does so.*)

STANLEY   I tell you something, Kurt, you're getting a
            bargain.

KURT   I'll tell you something, Stanley, I know we are.

HILDA   Will you gentlemen excuse us while Rose and I get
            dressed?

SVEN   The night is still young.

HILDA   The night might be, but I'm knackered.

ROSE   Excuse me, Sven.

            (HILDA *goes into the bedroom R and* ROSE *into the
            bedroom L.*)

KURT   Now, do you want the money paid into a foreign
            account?

NORMAN   Of course. That's the whole idea. We save a large
            percentage of tax and it's no skin off your nose.

KURT   Very well. Sven and I will sign, if anyone has a
            pen.

STANLEY   Here's a pen, Sven.

SVEN   Ta.

            (SVEN *takes the pen and signs.*)

KURT   Are you girls watching?

SABRINA   Sure.

KURT   Right. I'm signing and then as witnesses, you sign
            here, with your names, occupations and
            addresses.

            (SABRINA *looks at the contract.*)

SABRINA   Here, Val, look at these figures, thousands.

VALERIE   Some people make money the easy way.

(VALERIE *and* SABRINA *sign.*)

SVEN   So you are actually going to retire?

NORMAN   Yes, we deserve it. We've worked hard, haven't we, Stanley?

STANLEY   Quit while you're still young enough to enjoy life.

NORMAN   And our wives feel the same way.

(ROSE *enters in her dress.*)

ROSE   And what do your wives feel?

NORMAN   They're pleased to think we'll spend a lot more time at home.

ROSE   Don't bank on it.

(HILDA *enters.*)

HILDA   Has anyone seen my tights?

STANLEY   Don't all shout at once.

KURT   Ah, yes.

(KURT *pulls* HILDA'S *tights out of his pocket.*)

KURT   Here you are. You can undo the knots later.

HILDA   I don't remember that bit.

STANLEY   Just as well.

KURT   And where is the retirement going to take place?

STANLEY   We're taking our wives to Marbella.

HILDA   Lucky things.

NORMAN   We're buying two apartments in the Valparaiso Hill Club.

SVEN   (*laughing*) Valparaiso Hill Club?

NORMAN   D'you know it?

KURT	Know it? We own it. When you bring your wives down, we'd love to meet them.
HILDA	What? Oh my God.
ROSE	You own it!
SVEN	We know everyone worth knowing. We can introduce you to the social scene.
ROSE	Social scene?
HILDA	Oh no!
KURT	Oh yes!
SABRINA	Any chance of us getting a freebie down there?
KURT	As long as we do, you're always welcome.
SABRINA	Don't worry, Stan, if we happen to bump into you and the missus, we've never met before. All right?
STANLEY	Very thoughtful, Sabrina, much appreciated. But on second thoughts, we might revert to Plan B.
NORMAN	What plan's that?
STANLEY	We pay the full tax, stay in England and holiday in Bournemouth.
KURT	You make up your mind. The deal is done, and the next item on my agenda is to be shipwrecked on Coconut Island.

(KURT *takes* VALERIE'S *hand*.)

VALERIE	And man have I got some coconuts.

(KURT *and* VALERIE *exit*.)

SABRINA	Hey, big Svenda, d'you want to svend a little time with me?
SVEN	Vy not? Have you ever spent a night with an "Iron Man"?

SABRINA	No, but hope springs eternal.

(*They exit to* SVEN'S *bedroom.*)

STANLEY	So, are you ashamed of yourselves?
HILDA	No, why?
STANLEY	You've been prancing around this room, half naked.
ROSE	Nonsense, we were in lingerie.
STANLEY	What did you get up to with those two men?
HILDA	I'll tell you this. They never put a hand on us where we didn't want it.
ROSE	I can vouch for that.
NORMAN	I always knew I could trust you, love.
STANLEY	So nothing happened?
HILDA	We have nothing to be ashamed of.
STANLEY	Because Norman and I were worried for you.
HILDA	Any decent husband would be. Now, go and get the car.
STANLEY	I'll just have some prunes and custard before the journey. I'm starving!

(STANLEY *picks up the bowl and goes to sit in the chair.*)

HILDA	You haven't time for that.

(HILDA *takes the bowl from him and puts it on the small table by the chair.*)

ROSE	We'll stop at a service station for a burger and chips.

HILDA	Bring the car round to the front.
NORMAN	The road's up.
ROSE	Bring it around to the back. Use your imagination. You men can be very dumb at times.

(*They are all standing up ready to leave.*)

STANLEY	Not that dumb, we've got the contract signed.
HILDA	That's all you wanted.
STANLEY	It was until I saw you dressed as Hildegard. (*He nudges her.*) I'm looking forward to our retirement.
NORMAN	Me too.
HILDA	In that case, we better put you on multi-vitamins.
STANLEY	Right. From now on it's early to bed, and early to rise!
NORMAN	If we take enough of them.
HILDA	Pity about Spain.
STANLEY	Never mind, love.
ROSE	I'm quite relieved actually, when you see the type of person you might be mixing with. Fancy inviting those two tarts down there.
HILDA	There's no doubt about it, there's a lot to be said for Bournemouth.
ROSE	It suits us – we're more refined.
HILDA	Oh we are. We've got class.

(*Throwing tights into prunes and custard.*)

NORMAN	You can tell the proof's in the pudding!

(*Curtain.*)

Furniture and Property list

ON STAGE:

Sofa
Sideboard/Minibar containing whisky and beer
Armchair
Chairs
Coffee table
2 tables
Telephone
Framed pictures
Flowers

OFF STAGE:

Food trolley, with numerous sandwiches, canapés, prunes
and custard

PROPERTY:

Four tall glasses
Twelve short glasses
Tomato juice
Carrier bag containing two bottles of champagne and wine
(NORMAN)
Telephone book
Silver fruit bowl containing bananas
Bunch of grapes
Two "Iron Man" hats (Viking), one with two horns, the other
one horn (SVEN)
Mobile telephone (NORMAN)
Mobile telephone with Waltzing Matilda ring tone (VALERIE)
Bag (VALERIE)
Briefcase containing "Contracts" (NORMAN)
Briefcase (STANLEY)
Weekend bag (KURT)
Weekend bag (SVEN)
Two Schnapps bottles (SVEN)
"Harvey Nichols" carrier bag (ROSE)
Negligée (ROSE)
Towel and aerosol deodorant (KURT)

Furniture and Property list (cont.)

Pair of tights (KURT)
Sweater (ROSE)
Needle and thread (ROSE)
Dressing gown and turban (HILDA)
Sheet (KURT)
Dressing gown (KURT)
Twelve "fifty pound" notes (STANLEY)
Pen (STANLEY)

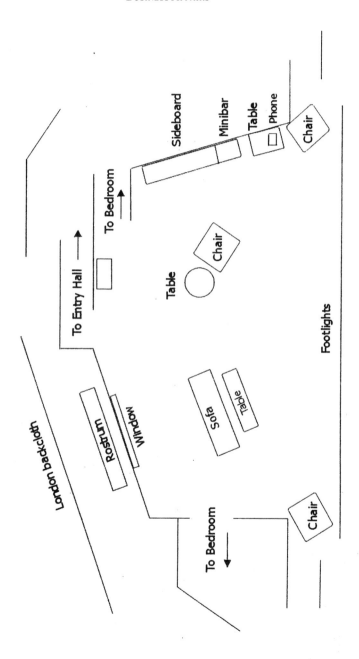